❧ CATO ❧
PAPERS ON
PUBLIC POLICY

Volume 2, 2012-2013

⤚ CATO ⤙
PAPERS ON
PUBLIC POLICY

Volume 2, 2012-2013

JEFFREY MIRON
Editor

JOHN A. ALLISON IV
Publisher

THOMAS A. FIREY
Managing Editor

PETER VAN DOREN
Associate Editor

SALLIE JAMES
Associate Editor

CATO
INSTITUTE

Washington, D.C.

Cato Papers on Public Policy, ISBN-10: 1-938048-92-X; ISBN-13: 978-1-938048-92-0. *CPPP* is published annually by the Cato Institute, a nonprofit, nonpartisan 501(c) (3) research organization based in Washington, D.C.

Correspondence regarding subscriptions, changes of address, procurement of back issues, advertising and marketing matters, and so forth, should be addressed to:

Publications Department
Cato Institute
1000 Massachusetts Avenue, N.W.
Washington, D.C. 20001

All other correspondence, including requests to quote or reproduce material, should be addressed to the editor.

To subscribe to *CPPP*, visit www.cato.org/store or call (800) 767-1241.

Printed in the United States of America.

Cato Institute
1000 Massachusetts Avenue, N.W.
Washington, D.C. 20001
www.cato.org

Publications Director: *David Lampo*
Marketing Director: *Robert Garber*
Circulation Manager: *Alan Peterson*
Cover: *Jon Meyers*

Contents

An Introduction to the 2012–2013 *Cato Papers on Public Policy* and Annual Conference

The goal of the *Cato Papers on Public Policy* and associated conference is to produce new, high-quality research on public policy and to make this research available to a broad audience consisting of academics, policymakers, and journalists.

The research intends to fill a gap in the work that addresses the pros and cons of government policies. Academics produce significant research that analyzes public policies, but much of that work is abstract, technical, and not immediately relevant to real-world policy debates. The *Cato Papers on Public Policy* will evaluate significant economic and social policies, using the techniques of modern economics. The papers will be less technical, on average, than a standard journal article, but more technical than a typical policy analysis. In a nutshell, the papers will aim to produce research that employs modern economic methodology but that is firmly focused on determining what policies are beneficial for the economy and society.

Jeffrey Miron
Editor, *Cato Papers on Public Policy*
Senior Fellow, Cato Institute
Senior Lecturer and Director of Undergraduate Studies, Harvard University

The French Gold Sink and the Great Deflation of 1929–32

Douglas A. Irwin

ABSTRACT

The gold standard was a key factor behind the Great Depression, but why did it produce such an intense worldwide deflation and associated economic contraction? While
the tightening of U.S. monetary policy in 1928 is often blamed for having initiated the
downturn, France increased its share of world gold reserves from 7 percent to 27 percent between 1927 and 1932, and failed to monetize most of this accumulation. This
created an artificial shortage of gold reserves and put other countries under significant
deflationary pressure. A simple calculation indicates that the United States and France
shared the blame (in a 60/40 split) for the withdrawal of gold from the rest of the
world and the onset of worldwide deflation in 1929. Counterfactual simulations indicate that world prices would have been stable during this period, instead of declining
calamitously, if the historical relationship between gold reserves and world prices
had continued. The deflation could have been avoided if central banks had simply
maintained their 1928 cover ratios.

Douglas A. Irwin is the John Sloan Dickey Third Century Professor of Arts and
Sciences and professor of economics at Dartmouth College. He is a research associate
of the National Bureau of Economic Research.

*The author thanks Michael Bordo, Barry Eichengreen, James Feyrer, Marc Flandreau, David
Friedman, Clark Johnson, Nancy Marion, Allan Meltzer, Michael Mussa, Martha Olney,
Randall Parker, Hugh Rockoff, Christina Romer, Marjorie Rose, Scott Sumner, and Peter
Temin for helpful comments and conversations.*

The French Gold Sink and the Great Deflation of 1929–32

1. INTRODUCTION

A large body of economic research has linked the gold standard to the length and severity of the Great Depression of the 1930s.[1] The gold standard's fixed-exchange rate regime transmitted financial disturbances across countries and prevented the use of monetary policy to address the economic crisis. Two compelling observations support this conclusion: countries not on the gold standard managed to avoid the Depression almost entirely, while countries on the gold standard did not begin to recover until they left it.[2]

While the link between the gold standard and the Great Depression is widely accepted, it begs the question of how the international monetary system produced such a monumental economic catastrophe. Structural flaws in the post–World War I gold standard and the fragility of international financial stability are often blamed for the problems of the period. However, it is not clear why such factors should have necessarily led to the massive price deflation experienced between 1929 and 1932 and the enormous economic difficulties associated with the decline in prices. In particular, there was no apparent shortage of gold in the 1920s and 1930s—worldwide gold reserves continued to expand—so it is not obvious why the system self-destructed and produced such a cataclysm.

Economic historians have traditionally singled out the United States for instigating the deflationary shock that led to the

---

[1] See Choudhri and Kochin (1980), Eichengreen and Sachs (1985), Hamilton (1988), Temin (1989), Bernanke and James (1991), Eichengreen (1992), and Bernanke (1995), among many other works.

[2] In terms of countries that were not on the gold standard, Spain and China stand out as examples of countries that largely avoided the economic collapse (Spain had a fiat currency and China was on a silver standard). Because countries on the gold standard chose to leave it at different times—the United Kingdom in 1931, the United States in 1933, and France in 1936—there is sufficient variation in country experiences to identify the recovery relationship.

3

worldwide Depression.[3] The standard explanation for the onset of the Depression is the tightening of U.S. monetary policy in early 1928, which led to gold inflows from the rest of the world that were sterilized by the Federal Reserve so that they did not affect the monetary base (Friedman and Schwartz 1963, Hamilton 1987). This forced other countries to tighten their monetary policies as well, without the benefit of a monetary expansion in the United States. From this initial deflationary impulse came banking panics and currency crises that merely reinforced the downward spiral of prices.

However, what is frequently overlooked—or mentioned only in passing—is the fact that France was doing almost exactly the same thing: accumulating gold reserves while failing to monetize them. Although its role is sometimes acknowledged, France's impact on the international monetary system is often believed to have been much smaller than that of the United States. In his famous League of Nations monograph, *The International Currency Experience*, Ragnar Nurkse (1944, 38–39) observed that "the French gold imports certainly aggravated the pressure of deflation in the rest of the world," but suggested that France's imports "contributed, though probably to a minor degree, to the forces making for depression in the rest of the world at the turning point of the business cycle in 1929–30." Similarly, Peter Temin (1989, 22) concludes that "American gold holdings were larger than those of the French, and the American influence on events was larger."

Yet France was accumulating gold reserves at a much more rapid rate than the United States. France's share of world gold reserves soared from 7 percent to 27 percent between 1926 and 1932. By contrast, although the U.S. share of world gold reserves rose slightly during a crucial period from 1928 to 1930, it generally fell in the late 1920s. The sheer size of the French gold accumulation in the late 1920s and early 1930s has led some economists to give its policies a closer look. Eichengreen (1990, 269–70) found that France's gold reserves were orders of magnitude larger than one would have predicted based on the country's economic attributes and concluded that "the exceptional demands for gold by the Federal Reserve and

<hr/>

[3] Milton Friedman and Anna Schwartz (1963, 360) argue that "the United States was in the van of the movement and not a follower." Similarly, Barry Eichengreen (1992, 222) states that "events in America were directly responsible for the slowdown in other parts of the world."

Banque de France placed downward pressure on global money supplies.... U.S. and French gold policies must therefore share the blame for exacerbating the monetary aspects of the Great Depression." Even Milton Friedman later said that, had he been fully aware of France's policy, he would have revised his view on the origins of the Great Depression.[4]

Scholars of French monetary history have even concluded that France deserves more blame than the United States for increasing the world's monetary stringency in the late 1920s and early 1930s. In *Gold, France, and the Great Depression,* Clark Johnson (1997, 147) contends that "while the United States did little to hinder the decline in world prices, especially after 1928, French policy can be charged with directly causing it." "That French gold policy aggravated the international monetary contraction from 1928 to 1932 is beyond dispute," Kenneth Mouré (2002, 180) argues. "The magnitude and timing of French gold absorption from mid-1928 to 1930 imposed a greater constraint on systemic monetary expansion than the gold accumulation in the United States during the same period."

Unfortunately, there is little quantitative evidence on the relative strength of the deflationary forces emanating from the United States and France as a result of their withdrawal of gold from the rest of the world. This paper seeks to address this question and begins by laying out some of the problems of the interwar gold standard and why it was vulnerable to a deflationary shock. The paper then turns to the factors behind the French gold accumulation and why it was not monetized. Finally, two counterfactual questions are raised: First, how much gold would have been freed up if the United States and France had kept only enough to cover their actual liabilities at their 1928 cover ratios?

---

[4] After re-reading the memoirs of Emile Moreau, the governor of the Bank of France, Friedman (1991, xii–xiii) said that he "would have assessed responsibility for the international character of the Great Depression somewhat differently" than he did originally in his *Monetary History* with Anna Schwartz, by laying some of the blame on France as well. Both the Federal Reserve and the Bank of France "were determined to prevent inflation and accordingly both sterilized the gold inflows, preventing them from providing the required increase in the quantity of money. . . . France's contribution to this process was, I now realize, much greater than we treated it as being in our [*Monetary*] *History*." In a 1998 interview, Friedman said, "[I]f I were rewriting [the *Monetary History*] now, I would paint a slightly different picture, one which made the great contraction and worldwide depression a consequence of the joint actions of both France and the U.S." (Parker 2002, 47)

Second, to what extent can those inactive, excess gold reserves account for the worldwide price deflation of 1929–32?

According to the calculations described below, the United States and France held excess gold, compared to 1928, equivalent to 5 percent of the world's gold reserves in 1929, 9 percent in 1930, and nearly 13 percent in 1931, when the gold standard began to fall apart. The United States and France contributed in almost equal proportions—about 60 percent to 40 percent—to the effective reduction in the world gold stock during those years. To assess the impact on world prices, the relationship between the world's wholesale prices and monetary gold stock is estimated for the period of the classical gold standard between 1870 and 1914. An out-of-sample forecast of the price level based on the actual changes in gold reserves suggests that, had the historical relationship between gold and prices continued, prices would have been roughly constant between 1929 and 1931 instead of declining 34 percent. The fact that the two countries kept such a large proportion of the world's gold stock effectively withdrawn from world circulation from 1929 to 1932 explains about 40 percent of the worldwide deflation at that time and may be indirectly responsible for some of the remainder.

These results support the view that France played a significant role in bringing about the great price deflation in the early 1930s. Contemporary observers at the time and scholars of the Great Depression today have been aware of France's gold position, but it remains a relatively neglected factor whose importance has not been fully appreciated. The findings presented here suggest that France deserves almost equal billing with the United States for having forced other countries to pursue a tighter monetary policy and thus initiating the worldwide deflationary spiral.

2. THE GOLD STANDARD AND FEARS OF DEFLATION

During World War I, most major countries abandoned the gold standard in order to use fiat currency to fund the war effort. As a result, those nations experienced high rates of inflation. The desire to bring inflation under control and restore monetary stability led most countries to plan on returning to the gold standard at some point after the war. Unfortunately, many of the international monetary difficulties of the late 1920s can be traced to decisions regarding the resumption of the gold standard in the mid-1920s.

Under the gold standard, the price level for goods and services was determined by the supply and demand for gold. The change in the price level was determined by the difference between the growth in the supply and the demand for gold: prices would rise if the world gold supply increased more rapidly than the demand for gold, whereas prices would fall if the demand for gold grew faster than the supply of gold.

Figure 1 illustrates these features by depicting the supply and demand for gold. The intersection of the world's gold supply and gold demand determines the relative price of gold in terms of other goods. In the short run, the world's supply of gold was fixed,

Figure 1
World Supply and Demand for Gold

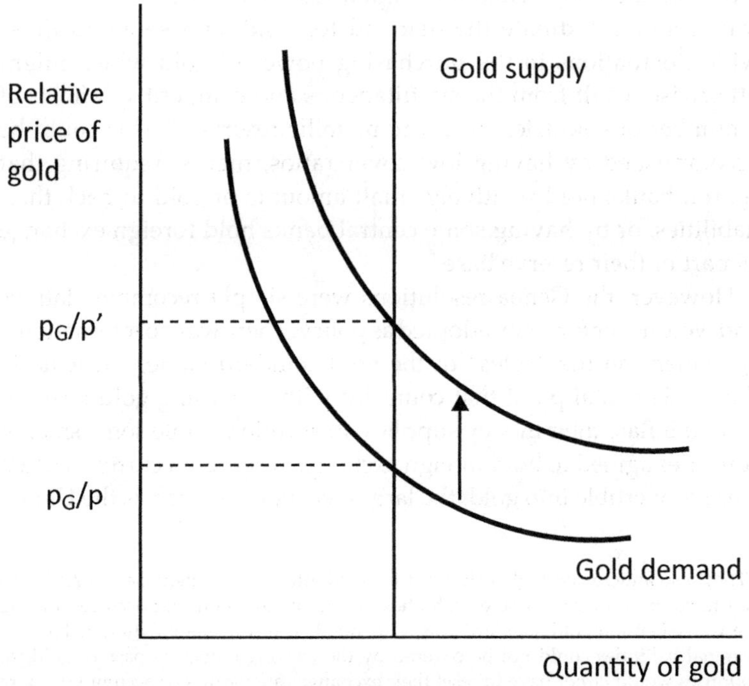

as indicated by the vertical supply line. Any increase in the demand for gold, such as the shift in Figure 1, would increase the relative price of gold. However, because the nominal price of gold was fixed in terms of national currencies, the adjustment would not take place through an increase in the price of gold but through a reduction in the price of other goods (deflation), as illustrated by the shift from p_G/p to p_G/p'.

Although ending inflation was a key motivation for returning to the gold standard, some leading economists of the day expressed the fear that a return to the gold standard could cause deflation. They feared that the slowing growth of gold production would make the supply of gold insufficient to keep up with the demand, which would increase if many countries sought to return to the gold standard and acquire gold reserves at the same time. Therefore, at the 1922 Genoa Conference on the international monetary system, Britain's Ralph Hawtrey and Sweden's Gustav Cassel encouraged countries to economize on their use of gold. Resolution No. 9 of the conference recommended that central banks "centralise and coordinate the demand for gold, and so avoid those wide fluctuations in the purchasing power of gold which might otherwise result from the simultaneous and competitive efforts of a number of countries to secure metallic reserves." This could be accomplished by having low cover ratios, that is, requiring that central banks hold relatively small amounts of gold to back their liabilities, or by having some central banks hold foreign exchange as part of their reserve base.[5]

However, the Genoa resolutions were simply recommendations and were never formally adopted as policy. There was no international agreement on the "rules" of the gold standard game, particularly the fundamental point that countries with increasing gold reserves should inflate their money supplies. In addition, while some smaller countries agreed to hold foreign exchange reserves in currencies that were convertible into gold, the largest economies, such as the United

---

[5] They also anticipated higher demand for gold after the war because central banks had to support a larger base of liabilities due to the inflation that occurred during the war when the gold standard was suspended. The wartime inflation meant that nominal liabilities could not be covered by the existing monetary base of gold, so countries would either have to reset their exchange rate parities or accumulate more gold reserves.

Figure 2
Number of Countries on the Gold Standard

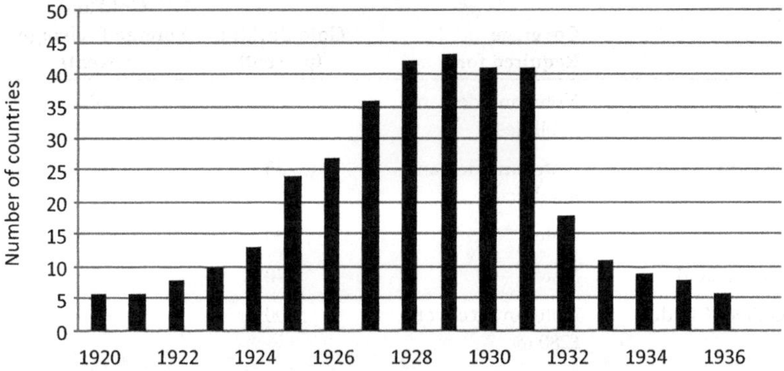

Source: Eichengreen (1992, 188–92).

States, Britain, and France, only held gold as reserves. Indeed, France rejected the gold exchange standard as inflationary and was firmly committed to a pure gold standard.[6]

Many countries began rejoining the gold standard following Britain's decision to do so in 1925. As Figure 2 shows, the number of countries on the gold standard increased significantly between 1924 and 1928.

As countries rejoined the gold standard, they established reserve requirements—or cover ratios—governing how much gold their central banks had to hold against their liabilities of currency in circulation and demand deposits. Such formal requirements were a departure from the classical gold standard. Furthermore, the cover ratios were asymmetric: while they specified a minimum level of

---

[6] As Mouré (2002, 188–89) notes: "The attitude of the Bank of France exemplified the asymmetry and the deflationary bias of the gold standard. The bank rejected the gold exchange standard as a dilution of the gold standard that promoted an over-expansion of credit. . . .. The Bank of France set itself resolutely against measures to increase domestic monetary circulation and prices."

CATO PAPERS ON PUBLIC POLICY

Table 1
Legal Reserve Requirements

	Coverage Required for	Gold Backing (percent)	Gold and Foreign Exchange (percent)
Belgium	Notes and demand liabilities	30	40*
France	Notes and demand liabilities	35	—
Germany	Notes	30	40
Switzerland	Notes	40	—
United Kingdom	Notes in excess of £280 m	100	—
United States	Deposits	35	—
	Notes	40	

* Belgium shifted from the gold exchange standard to the gold standard in August 1930.
Source: *Federal Reserve Bulletin*, August 1930, p. 502.

gold reserves below which central banks could not go, they did not set a maximum level beyond which banks could not go. (See Table 1.)

With the international monetary system lacking an agreed upon framework, the resurrected gold standard stood on a precarious foundation. Throughout the 1920s, Cassel repeatedly warned of an impending shortage of gold and the possibility of worldwide price deflation (Irwin 2011). In lectures delivered at Columbia University in May 1928, Cassel (1928, 44) argued that "the great problem before us is how to meet the growing scarcity of gold which threatens the world both from increased demand and from diminished supply." While little could be done about the projected slowing of growth in the supply of gold, Cassel proposed to remedy the imbalance by restricting the monetary demand for gold: "[O]nly if we succeed in doing this can we hope to prevent a permanent fall of the general price level and a prolonged and worldwide depression which would inevitably be connected with such a fall in prices."

Cassel (1928, 98–99) believed that without international cooperation to stabilize the value of gold, the result would

> obviously be a general and ruthless competition for gold, a
> consequent continual rise in the value of gold, and a corre-
> sponding world-wide economic depression for an unlimited
> future. A very disagreeable consequence of such a movement
> in the value of gold would be a general aggravation of all
> debts contracted in a gold standard, doubtless in many cases
> followed by an incapacity to pay debts or a refusal to do
> so. We must remember that the great part of the world that
> would have to suffer from such a development has a very
> powerful weapon of defense. This weapon is simply the abo-
> lition of gold as a monetary standard.

As is evident from the rapid decline in countries on the gold standard starting in late 1931, Cassel was prescient in predicting that
countries would abandon the gold standard if the stress of deflation
was too severe.

As it happened, Cassel's fears about an insufficient supply of gold
were misplaced: forecasts of slowing gold production were off the
mark and the supply of monetary gold continued to expand through
the early 1930s. As Figure 3 shows, the supply of gold reserves continued to grow through the late 1920s and into the 1930s. In fact,
world gold reserves increased 19 percent between 1928 and 1933.
But his fears about the increasing monetary demand for gold were
entirely realized.

2.1 The Distribution of Gold Reserves

While there was no major problem with the supply of gold,
there was a problem with the demand for gold when many countries returned to the gold standard at the same time. In particular, the distribution of gold reserves changed dramatically as the
Bank of France began to accumulate gold at a rapid rate. Between
1923 and 1926, France's share of world gold reserves was stable
and virtually the same as Britain's. However, after the de facto
stabilization of the franc in 1926 (de jure in 1928), France's share
took off, growing from 7 percent of world reserves in 1926 to
27 percent in 1932. By 1932, France held nearly as much gold as
the United States, though its economy was only about a fourth
of the size of the United States. Together, the United States and

Figure 3
World Gold Reserves, 1925–32

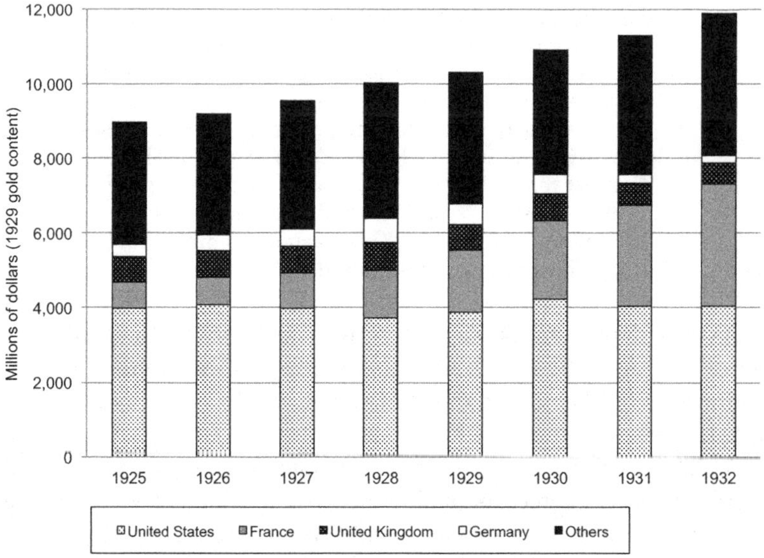

Source: Hardy (1936, 92).

France held more than 60 percent of the world's monetary gold stock in 1932.[7]

What was driving changes in the international distribution of gold reserves? To some extent, changes were driven by the exchange rate at which countries rejoined the gold standard. Some countries restored their prewar parity, while others took inflation into account and refixed at a depreciated exchange rate. The reconstructed gold standard started off on the wrong foot in 1925 when Britain rejoined it at an exchange rate that overvalued the pound (Moggridge 1969). This not only harmed the competitive position of export industries but also meant that the British balance of payments remained in a fragile state. The balance of

[7] Eichengreen (1990, 264) finds that U.S. monetary gold stocks were two to three times, and French gold stocks were three to five times, what would be predicted on the basis of estimated central bank reserve demand from a cross section of countries.

payments weakness required the Bank of England to maintain a tight monetary policy to support the pound, keeping interest rates high and thereby diminishing domestic investment. This kept economic growth in check and made it difficult for Britain to reduce its already high level of unemployment. As a result, Britain suffered through a low-grade deflation from 1925 until the country left gold in 1931.

Meanwhile, after enduring a traumatic bout of inflation in 1924–26, France stabilized the franc at an undervalued rate. There is some debate about whether the undervaluation was deliberate or not.[8] French policymakers certainly debated which exchange rate the country should choose. Once the franc had been stabilized, foreign exchange markets put upward pressure on the franc as confidence in its value was restored. Finance Minister Raymond Poincaré wanted to allow the franc to appreciate before formally establishing the peg to gold, while Bank of France Governor Emile Moreau wanted to resist the exchange market pressure and keep the franc at the lower rate. France formalized its adoption of the gold standard with the Monetary Law of June 1928, which officially restored convertibility of the franc in terms of gold at the rate set in December 1926.

The evolution of gold reserves in Figure 4 reveals much about the monetary policies and exchange rate choices in the major countries. The United States lost reserves (relative to other countries) between 1926 and 1928 in part because of large capital exports to Europe. This foreign lending was largely directed to Germany, which used the loans to repay reparations to Britain and France, which in turn repaid its war loans from the United States. These capital flows also allowed Germany to rebuild its gold reserves, which steadily increased between 1923 and 1928. France began accumulating gold reserves once the franc was stabilized at an undervalued rate in late 1926, while Britain with its overvalued pound had to make do with an ever smaller share of the world's gold stock.

However, when the Federal Reserve began to tighten policy in early 1928, U.S. foreign lending dried up, the net export of gold reversed itself, and the U.S. share of reserves stabilized in 1929 and 1930. As American lending came to a halt, Germany's gold reserve position began to deteriorate. The United States began losing reserves to other countries again in 1931 and 1932, after Britain left the gold standard in September 1931.

---

[8] See Sicsic (1992) and Mouré (1996) for differing views.

Figure 4
Share of World Gold Reserves

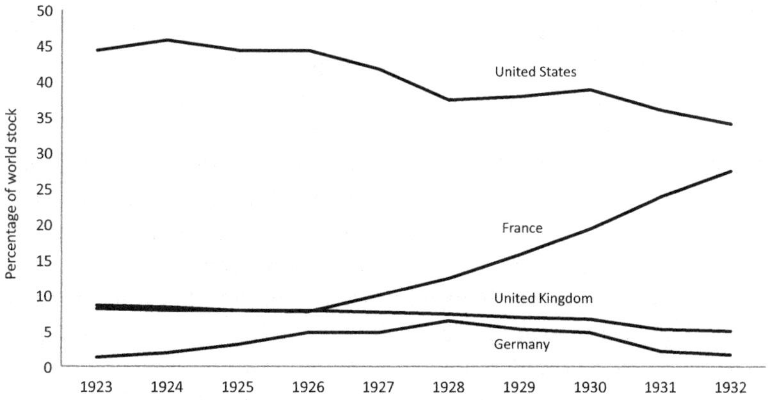

Source: Hardy (1936, 93).

Thus, France's stabilization in 1926 and America's tightening of monetary policy in 1928 allowed the two countries to accumulate and retain a large share of the world's gold reserves. This reduced the absolute amount of gold reserves available for the rest of the world, as Table 2 shows. In 1928, the flow of gold to France and from the United States almost exactly offset each other, allowing the gold reserves of the rest of the world to grow by 4 percent. In December 1928, world gold reserves were 5 percent larger than they had been in December 1927; France gained 3 percentage points of that increase, the United States lost 2 percentage points, allowing the rest of the world to gain 4 percentage points.

The situation changed in 1929 when, instead of offsetting one another, the United States joined France in attracting gold away from the rest of the world. As a result, the rest of the world lost 3 percent of the world stock. The same thing happened in 1930 as well. In 1931, the world gold stock rose 3 percent, but France accumulated 8 percentage points, taking 2 percent of the world gold stock away from the United States and 3 percent from the rest of the world.

Table 2
Gold Reserves: Percentage Change from Previous Year

	Total World Gold Reserves	Absorption by (percentage of total world reserves)		
		United States	France	Rest of World
December 1928	+5	−2	+3	+4
December 1929	+3	+2	+4	−3
December 1930	+6	+3	+5	−2
December 1931	+3	−2	+8	−3
December 1932	+5	+0	+3	+3
Cumulative percentage change from December 1927				
December 1931	+18	+1	+21	−4
December 1932	+24	+1	+24	0

Source: Board of Governors of the Federal Reserve System (1943, 544−45).
Note: Final three columns may not sum to first column because of rounding.

The cumulative effect was astounding. In December 1932, world gold reserves were 24 percent larger than they had been in December 1927. However, France absorbed almost every ounce of the additional gold, leaving the rest of the world with no net increase. Watching this trend unfold, John Maynard Keynes (1932, 83) could not resist this biting remark: "And, when the last gold bar in the world has been safely lodged in the Bank of France, that will be the appropriate moment for the German Government to announce that one of their chemists has just perfected the technique for making the stuff at 6d. an ounce." The United States seems to have been less of a problem because it was not systematically accumulating gold throughout the period, although it did so during the crucial years of 1929 and 1930.

The deflationary pressure that this redistribution of gold put on other countries is remarkable. In 1929, 1930, and 1931, the rest of the world lost the equivalent of about 8 percent of the world's gold stock, an enormous proportion—15 percent—of the rest of the world's December 1928 reserve holdings. Gardner (1932, 63) summed up the situation this way: "The picture of the five years ending 1930 may perhaps be drawn in one sentence thus: A world, returning to the gold standard and unable to tap the surplus gold of the United

15

States, lost the bulk of its new supplies to France, notwithstanding the fact that these new supplies were exceptionally large because of the flow from special and non-recurrent sources."

2.2 Monetary Neutralization

This massive redistribution of gold reserves might not have been a problem for the world economy if the United States and France had been monetizing the gold inflows. That would have been playing by the rules of the game of the classical gold standard: countries receiving gold inflows would have had a monetary expansion that would have balanced the monetary contraction in countries losing gold.

But as already noted, there were no agreed-upon rules of the game in the interwar gold standard. Both France and the United States were effectively neutralizing—or not monetizing—the inflows to ensure that they did not have an expansionary effect. The United States was explicitly sterilizing the gold inflows by conducting open market operations (purchases of Treasury securities) to offset their monetary impact.[9] France was not explicitly sterilizing the gold inflows, but the inflows failed to have much expansionary effect on the country's monetary stance for reasons that will be discussed below. As a result, this asymmetry—countries receiving gold failed to expand, while countries losing gold had to contract—gave the international monetary system a severe deflationary bias.

The neutralization of gold inflows is implicit in the cover ratios presented in Figure 5. The cover ratio is the ratio of central bank gold reserves to its domestic liabilities (notes in circulation and demand deposits). If countries followed the rules of the game and monetized gold inflows and outflows alike, the country's cover ratio would have been roughly constant. Once again, France stands out in comparison to the other countries. As mandated by the Monetary Law of 1928, the Bank of France was required to back a minimum of 35 percent

---

[9] "The international effects were severe and the transmission rapid, not only because the gold-exchange standard had rendered the international financial system more vulnerable to disturbances, but also because the United States did not follow gold-standard rules," Friedman and Schwartz (1963, 361) note. "We did not permit the inflow of gold to expand the U.S. money stock. We not only sterilized it, we went much further. Our money stock moved perversely, going down as the gold stock went up. . . . The result was that other countries not only had to bear the whole burden of adjustment but also were faced with continued additional disturbances in the same direction, to which they had to adjust."

Figure 5
Cover Ratios of Major Central Banks, 1928–32

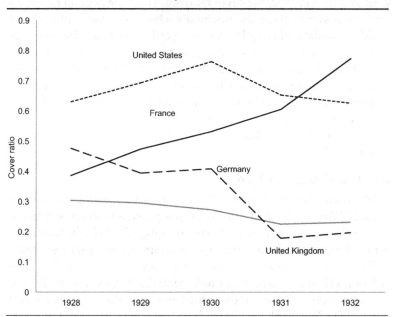

Source: Calculated from the Board of Governors of the Federal Reserve System (1943).
Note: Data are for December of each year.

of its liabilities with gold, although the bank wanted a minimum of 40 percent in practice (Mouré 1991, 47–48). This is about where the cover ratio was in December 1928. Of course, the lower bound was a floor, but there was no ceiling or maximum cover ratio beyond which the bank was forbidden to go. By 1930, France's cover ratio rose to more than 50 percent. In January 1931, the cover ratio reached 55 percent, at which point the Bank of France considered but rejected a proposal to suspend its gold purchases (Mouré 2002, 188). By 1932, the cover ratio had risen to nearly 80 percent. France was well on its way to having 100 percent base money, in which all of the central bank liabilities were backed one-for-one with gold in its vault.

The path of the U.S. cover ratio is also consistent with the previous discussion of monetary policy. The U.S. cover ratio rose in 1929 and

1930 as the United States accumulated gold after the Federal Reserve raised interest rates in 1928. However, when the United States lost gold in 1931 and 1932, the cover ratio fell. Thus, the Federal Reserve's policy was symmetric: it did not inflate when gold was coming in and it did not deflate when gold was going out. Once again, by this measure, U.S. policy was somewhat tighter in 1929 and 1930, but somewhat looser in 1931 and 1932, with regard to the rest of the world, whereas France's policy was consistently tight throughout this period.

Meanwhile, Germany's cover ratio fell sharply in 1929 but stabilized in 1930. Britain's cover ratio was the lowest of the three and declined slightly as the Bank of England struggled to keep hold of its existing gold reserves.

2.3 Explaining French Policy

What was driving French gold and monetary policy during this period? Was the Bank of France simply passive with respect to the gold inflows, or was it actively encouraging it? And what accounts for the failure to monetize the rapidly accumulating gold reserves?

The answer depends in part on the particular time period considered. When the franc was finally stabilized in December 1926, it was—or soon became—undervalued in comparison to other major currencies. The Bank of France had to engage in large-scale foreign exchange intervention to prevent the appreciation of the franc. France's foreign exchange holdings rose from $50 million in November 1926 to $777 million by the end of May 1927 (Clarke 1967, 111).

However, this intervention, involving the sale of millions of francs to purchase pounds and dollars, did not have an inflationary effect in France. The stabilization of government finances enabled it to reap budget surpluses or led to capital inflows driven by the purchase of government securities, which were used to repay advances from the Bank of France. These budget surpluses, deposited at the Bank of France, removed the francs from circulation and were a deflationary offset to the sale of francs on foreign exchange markets.[10] As Nurkse

---

[10] "In effect, much of the cash that was pumped into the market by the Bank of France's purchases of foreign exchange was mopped up by Treasury funding issues, the proceeds of which were employed to reduce the government's short-term debt to the central bank. The authorities thus shifted government debt from the central bank to the market and achieved the same results that would have been attained through central bank open market sales." Clark (1967, 111).

(1944, 77) pointed out, from the end of 1926 until mid-1928, two-thirds of the gold inflow was "neutralized" by the reduction in the bank's holding of government debt. (He used the term "neutralization" rather than "sterilization" because he regarded it as automatic and not a deliberate policy.)[11]

However, the Bank of France became concerned about its rapidly growing foreign exchange reserves and began selling pounds and dollars for gold from the Bank of England and the Federal Reserve. This was the beginning of France's gold accumulation. The gold drain alarmed officials at the Bank of England, and in June 1927 the Bank of France reached an accommodation with Britain to stop its gold purchases and to keep its sterling reserves at the existing level.[12] The Bank of France then dealt with the situation by buying forward contracts on foreign exchange (selling pounds and dollars for francs now with the promise to repurchase the pounds and dollars a year later). These swaps temporarily kept the francs out of circulation and bought the bank a year of time.

Around the time these forward contracts came due, the Monetary Law of 1928 took effect. The law tied the hands of the Bank of France in several important ways. The bank was required to maintain gold reserves of at least 35 percent of sight liabilities (notes and demand deposits). In addition, the bank no longer had the legal authority to purchase foreign exchange and henceforth could only acquire gold. Finally, the bank was prohibited from engaging in open market operations, so it could never again monetize government deficits.

As a result, the Bank of France could no longer acquire foreign exchange instead of gold. Gold continued to flow into the country

---

[11] As Nurkse (1944, 77) notes:

> The reduction in the government's debt to the Bank was at bottom equivalent to an open-market operation, since it meant a shift in the holding of pre-existing government debt from the Bank to the market. Unlike an ordinary open-market operation, however, it did not come about at the Bank's initiative; and above all, being a "sale" instead of a purchase, it took place in the opposite direction to that which the "rules of the game" would have required. The "rules of the game" . . . would have required an inflation of domestic credit to reinforce the effects of the gold inflow; but the country had just emerged from a period of inflation and was not in the mood for more.

[12] Accominotti (2009) examines the Bank of France's management of its foreign exchange portfolio.

for several reasons. France was an undermonetized economy with a shortage of currency. Banks accommodated the demand for currency by withdrawing funds from overseas accounts, selling their pound and dollar assets for gold, which they would then turn over to the Bank of France for currency (Balogh 1930; Hawtrey 1932). Financial institutions were reluctant to discount bills at the Bank of France, which competed with them for commercial business. As the 1930 annual report of the Bank of France noted, "when on various occasions they [banks] were confronted with large demands for francs in their own market during 1930, they naturally preferred to repatriate part of those unproductive [foreign] balances rather than have recourse to the rediscount facilities obtainable at the Bank of France" (*Federal Reserve Bulletin*, March 1931, 146).[13] In addition, the bank could not conduct open market operations to inject additional currency into the financial system. Furthermore, particularly as economic troubles appeared in central Europe in mid-1931, there was capital flight to France as the franc was considered a safe asset.

A closer look at the balance sheet of the Bank of France indicates that it was not sterilizing the gold inflows in the classic sense of reducing domestic assets to offset the increase in foreign assets.[14] As Table 3 indicates, the bank continued to accumulate domestic assets even as its foreign asset holdings grew. The bank's total assets grew 29 percent between 1928 and 1932, although this understates the growth because the bank did not treat foreign exchange as part of its monetary base; total assets of gold and domestic assets grew 102 percent.

Despite this growth in the monetary base, the money supply was essentially unchanged over this period. The implicit money

[13] As the deputy controller of finance for the British Treasury, Sir Frederick Leith-Ross, put it, "the gold is not imported into France for commercial purposes; it is imported in order to be handed over to the Bank of France against francs. The movement of gold appears therefore to be due to a constantly recurring need for additional franc resources and if the movement is to be prevented, it will be necessary to ascertain what causes this shortage of francs." Royal Institute for International Affairs (1932, 53–54).

[14] Balogh (1930, 442) said that "those who make the charge of willful hoarding mistake conscious tactics for the shortcomings of the French banking system." Clarke (1967, 167) argued that the failure to monetize the gold inflows stemmed "from French institutional arrangements and financial policies—from the Bank of France's lack of authority to conduct open market operations, from the commercial banks' reluctance to discount at the central bank, and from the piling up at the central bank of surplus Treasury and other official receipts from the public."

Table 3
Bank of France's Balance Sheet, 1928–32
Millions of francs, end of December of each year

Year	Foreign Assets		Domestic Assets	Total Liabilities (monetary base)	Money Supply (M2)	Money Multiplier
	Gold	Foreign Exchange				
1928	32.0	32.7	19.9	84.6	161.7	1.91
1929	41.7	25.9	22.4	90.0	161.5	1.80
1930	53.6	26.2	23.2	103.0	170.2	1.65
1931	68.8	21.1	25.8	115.8	164.7	1.42
Percent Change (1928–31)	+115	−35	+30	+37	+2	—

Sources: Board of Governors of the Federal Reserve System (1943, 641–42); M2 from Patat and Lutfalla (1990, Table A2).

multiplier dropped and offset the increase in high powered money. Figure 6 depicts France's reserves of gold, gold and foreign exchange, and money supply (M2). Simply put, the growth in the bank's gold reserves was not getting translated into the nation's money and credit.

And fiscal policy continued to exert a contractionary impact. Budget surpluses were deposited at the Bank of France and built up as idle balances because of the fear of monetization and inflation, as occurred before the 1926 stabilization. Hawtrey (1932, 24) noted that the repatriation of foreign capital "was mainly the result of big government loans. The government borrowed paper francs from the public and cancelled them by repaying advances to the Bank of France. The public, being short of paper francs, economized on imports and thereby acquired sufficient foreign exchange to extract a fresh supply of currency from the bank."

To some extent, the falling money multiplier was beyond the direct control of the Bank of France. Eichengreen (1986) examines the variety of institutional and legal constraints on the ability of the Bank of France to translate its expanding gold reserves into the money supply. Those policies were designed to tie the hands of the bank and prevent a reoccurrence of the inflation that the country had experienced earlier in the 1920s. Under the Monetary Law of 1928, the bank

Figure 6
France's Monetary Indicators, 1926–32

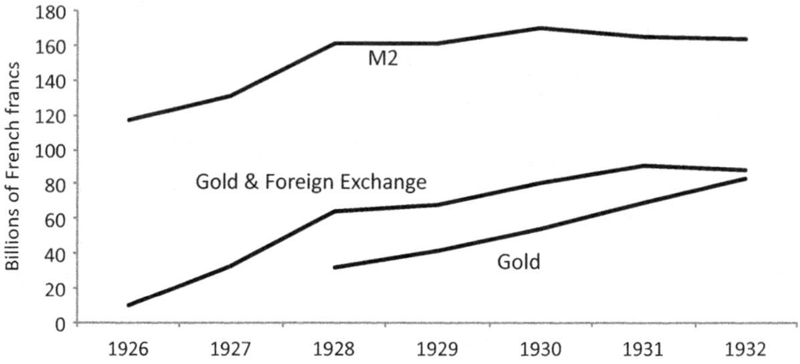

Sources: Patat and Lutfalla (1990, Table A2); Mouré (1991, 55–56).

was restricted in its ability to undertake open market operations to ease the monetary situation and slow the gold inflows. The French banking system was also notoriously inefficient at transforming reserves into francs. Given these restrictions on the Bank of France and the institutional environment, Eichengreen (1986) concludes that few policies (except open market operations, had they been permitted) could have stopped the French gold accumulation.[15]

Bernanke and Mihov (2000, 139–40, 148–50) make a qualified defense of the Bank of France. They observe that "the falling money multiplier combined with the Bank of France's movement from foreign exchange reserves to gold accounts for essentially the entire nullification of the effect of the gold inflows on the domestic money supply." Furthermore, the ratio of the monetary base to international reserves was basically unchanged, according to the data they

---

[15] Eichengreen (1986) argues that "France's painful experience with inflation in the early 1920s was directly responsible for the adoption of the stringent regulations which prevented the central bank from intervening to prevent the accumulation of gold." He suggests that "viewing French attitudes in their historical context sheds more light on the actions of policymakers than do allegations of obstinacy or of failure to understand the workings of the international monetary system."

present. Therefore, they conclude that "the actions of the Bank of France are difficult to fault. . . . [T]he Bank of France conducted policy almost entirely according to the gold standard's 'rules of the game.'" Unfortunately, Bernanke and Mihov find that the base-reserve ratio (the inverse of the cover ratio) was stable because they include foreign exchange reserves as part of France's reserves (see their footnote 6 on page 143). Yet France never adhered to the gold exchange standard, and indeed explicitly rejected it, and its cover ratio was far from constant during this period, as Figure 5 indicates. Therefore, the conclusion that France adhered to the rules of the game is inaccurate.[16]

Taken together, Figures 3, 4, and 5 illustrate why France was viewed as a "gold sink" by contemporary observers. This makes a plausible case that France's gold and monetary policies from 1928 to 1932 may have been as problematic for the world as American gold and monetary policies. Before turning to empirical evidence, the international reaction to France's gold accumulation is worth briefly considering.

2.4 The International Reaction

The growing French accumulation of gold soon became a source of international concern. In January 1929, John Maynard Keynes acknowledged that he had been wrong not to take more seriously Cassel's warnings about the gold standard's problems. Keynes (1929) argued that "a difficult, and even a dangerous, situation is developing" because

> there may not be enough gold in the world to allow all the central banks to feel comfortable at the same time. In this event they will compete to get what gold there is—which means that each will force his neighbor to tighten credit in self-protection, and that a protracted deflation will

---

[16] Bernanke and Mihov (2000, 148–50) temper their claim with this statement: "This is not to claim that French monetary policies were not bad, even disastrous, for the world as a whole: in particular, the large gold inflows induced by the conversion of foreign exchange and the switch by French citizens from deposits to currency put major pressure on other gold standard countries to tighten their monetary policies. However, the damage done by French policies lay to a much greater degree in the government's choice of monetary regime—its commitment to the gold standard, with minimal use of foreign exchange reserves—than in the Bank of France's implementation of that regime."

> restrict the world's economic activity, until, at long last, the
> working classes of every country have been driven down
> against their impassioned resistance to a lower money
> wage.

The recent behavior of the Bank of France "cannot help but cause an artificial shortage of gold," he noted. "The question of the sufficiency of the world's gold supplies in the abundance or scarcity of credit in the world's business lies, therefore, for the near future in the hands of the Bank of France."

By mid-1929, wholesale prices around the world began to fall and the deflationary spiral had begun. In March 1930 testimony before the Macmillan Committee, Keynes argued that the situation was reversible: "If . . . the United States and France were to declare that they would do everything reasonably in their power not to take more gold for a year or two, and, if practicable to lose ten percent of their present holdings, one would say that, in addition to other expedients, would make the position almost safe. I am absolutely confident that we could bring back the level of prices to what it was a couple of years ago." However, the problem was that "it is very doubtful how far the Bank of France is aware either of the existence of the problem or of the nature of the solution" (Keynes 1981, 154).

The Bank of France consistently denied that its policies were responsible for the inflow of gold. The 1929 annual report of the bank noted that "we never took the initiative in acquiring gold by means of foreign bills. We were obliged, in fulfillment of our obligation to regulate the currency, to accept all gold of foreign origin which was offered to us over the counter for francs, but we did not at any time intervene in the exchange market to accelerate the pace of these gold imports" (*Federal Reserve Bulletin*, March 1930, 113). Instead, the gold inflows were said to reflect confidence in French economic policies.[17]

---

[17] Sicsic (1993) notes that the capital inflows arose from the repatriation of capital by French residents after the stabilization became credible. Yet as Mouré (2002, 187) points out, this still created problems for the international financial system because even if all the gold coming back was repatriated capital, it had left the country without producing any decline in French gold reserves while it returned to France by delivering gold from the rest of the world.

French policymakers also denied accusations that they were sterilizing gold inflows.[18] Finance Minister Paul Reynaud (1933, 258) pointed out that new francs had been issued in almost equal value to the amount of gold accumulated between 1928 and 1932 "as is required by the gold standard system." (Reynaud failed to note that a decline in commercial banks' deposits had largely offset the increase in note issue.) He and other bank officials, such as Charles Rist (1932), argued that the Monetary Law of 1928 tied the hands of the bank in terms of its ability to pursue a more expansionary monetary policy.

Yet even if they could have pursued a more expansionary policy, French policymakers were not inclined to do anything much differently. Despite the expanding reserve base, the Bank of France did not want to pursue an "inflationary" monetary policy, so it took measures to limit the impact of gold on monetary circulation. French officials were satisfied with the situation and did not see why any changes should be made. They were particularly pleased with the rising cover ratio because it provided a cushion against capital flight. "It would have been extremely imprudent of the Bank to put all its gold to work, even had that been possible," Reynaud (1933, 258–60) argued. "The Bank of France has the duty to be forearmed against the possibility of a sudden withdrawal of foreign funds. . . . It is the duty of the Bank of France to guard against this danger by maintaining, not a sterile gold reserve, but a margin of available credit, so that it may intervene at an opportune moment and so far as possible modify the effect produced by the withdrawal of foreign capital."

As one might expect, French policy led to conflict with British officials, who were well aware that France's policy was making its own adjustment difficult in view of the overvalued pound. In January–February 1931, British officials consulted with their French counterparts to see if France would address its monetary situation. French officials insisted that the gold inflow demonstrated market confidence in its good policies, that they had done nothing deliberate to increase the gold inflow, and that there was nothing that they could do to stop it (Mouré 2002, 183–86). They put the burden on Britain to

---

[18] Reynaud (1933, 260) also tried to cast French policy in a favorable light in comparison to the Federal Reserve: "Unlike the United States, the Bank of France has never tried to neutralize the influx of gold into France. It felt that such a policy, by maintaining artificial credit conditions, would actually have stimulated the import of gold and aggravated the monetary difficulties of other countries."

raise interest rates further if they wished to attract gold. The French explanation failed to satisfy the British Treasury. As Ralph Hawtrey put it, "We complain of the drain of gold because it tends to cause a monetary contraction here and in the rest of the world, and Monsieur Escallier's reply is that we can prevent the drain of gold if we choose to effect a monetary contraction!" (Mouré 1991, 63)

British officials at the League of Nations also tried to raise the issue of the so-called maldistribution of gold and succeeded in establishing a Gold Delegation to investigate the problem. But the topic proved so controversial that the League was unable to address it head-on (Clavin and Wessels 2004). The Gold Delegation issued an interim report in September 1930 and concluded that "the problem of the distribution of gold is thus one of great importance. . . . [I]f the distribution of gold is the result of excessive or abnormal competition by a few countries, or if it has the effect of sterilizing important amounts of monetary stocks, serious consequences will arise affecting the general level of prices" (League of Nations 1930a, 17). The delegation proposed to alleviate the problem of excess demand for monetary gold through an international agreement for a coordinated reduction in cover ratios.[19]

Yet no serious efforts were made in 1930 or 1931 to address the gold situation. In September 1931, after Britain faced mounting losses in gold reserves as a result of the European financial crisis in mid-1931, Keynes argued that the United States and France were "primarily responsible for the disastrous fall in the level of world prices."

> The whole world is heartily sick of the selfishness and folly with which the international gold standard is being worked. Instead of being a means of facilitating international trade, the gold standard has become a curse laid upon the economic life of the world. It is not necessary to go into academic questions as to how far the fall in the world level of prices has been brought about by a worldwide shortage of gold. It is only necessary to look at the present distribution of the world's gold stocks. (Keynes 1981, 600)

---

[19] As a dissenting member of the Gold Delegation, Cassel (1932) bluntly stated what the more diplomatic League of Nations report could not say, that it was "especially remarkable that the Bank of France has consistently and unnecessarily acquired enormous amounts of gold without troubling in the least about the consequences that such a procedure is bound to have on the rest of the world."

Keynes called for an international gold conference to address the issue:

> This gold conference has to be put forward to America and France as an act of common sense and prudence, as a means of saving the economic world from the disaster which will surely overtake it if the slump is to be prolonged by a universal deflation policy....We must make it plain to our friends on the gold standard that, if they refuse to play the game according to the rules, this is not to be made a compelling reason for reducing the standard of life in this country for a generation. If, as a result of the conference's failure, we were to leave the gold standard system, this would be preferable to the deflation policy with which the Coalition Government intends to launch this country in the race for economic suicide. (Keynes 1981, 602–3)

In fact, time had run out, and Britain left the gold standard just days after Keynes published this piece.

3. QUANTIFYING THE EXCESSIVE GOLD HOLDINGS BY FRANCE AND THE UNITED STATES

As noted earlier, there has been surprisingly little work done on the amount of gold withdrawn from world circulation by the United States and France and its effect on world prices.[20] To assess the contribution of American and French monetary policies to the worldwide deflation of the early 1930s, two counterfactual questions will be posed. First, how much excess gold was being held by the two countries? Second, to what extent can that excess gold accumulation explain the worldwide price deflation of the early 1930s?

The impact of the American and French monetary policies starting in 1928 can be assessed by calculating how much gold was sitting "inactive" in the vaults of the Federal Reserve and the Bank of France—that is, how much gold would have been freed up if the United States and France had kept only enough to cover their actual liabilities at their

---

[20] Eichengreen (1990) found that if the U.S. and French shares of gold reserves had been at levels predicted by their economic characteristics, the gold reserves of other countries could have *doubled*. And "assuming that central banks were concerned to retain some proportion between their reserves and domestic liabilities," Eichengreen (1990, 264) concluded, "this redistribution of reserves would have provided considerable scope for an expansion of money supplies."

1928 cover ratio. Given that the world economy seemed to be doing reasonably well in 1928, the year in which the Federal Reserve began to tighten monetary policy and the Bank of France officially began operating under the new Monetary Law, that year will be taken as a benchmark. Specifically, we can start in June 1928 when the Bank of France first published its balance sheet under the new monetary regime.

The key assumption is that the two countries maintain their cover ratio—the ratio of gold reserves to domestic liabilities (notes in circulation and demand deposits)—at their June 1928 levels in subsequent years. (France's cover ratio was 40.45 percent on June 25, 1928.) Letting G stand for the gold reserves and L for domestic liabilities, the reserve ratio r for the 1928 benchmark can be calculated as $r_{28} = G_{28} \div L_{28}$, as depicted in Figure 5. The amount of excess gold held in 1929 can be calculated as $G_{29} - r_{28} \times L_{29}$, where $r_{28} \times L_{29}$ is the amount of gold required in 1929 to maintain the same 1928 cover ratio for the actual amount of outstanding liabilities in 1929. This can be calculated for subsequent months and years in the same way.

Figure 7 presents the monthly excess gold holdings of the United States and France as a share of the world's gold stock from June 1928.

Figure 7
Effective Reduction in World's Monetary Gold Stock, 1929–31

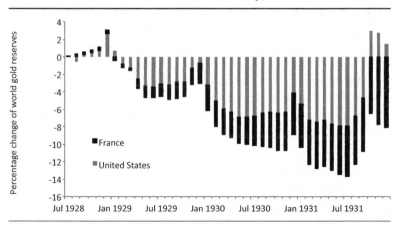

Source: Author's calculations. See text.

These countries did not have a contractionary impact on other countries for the remainder of that year. The United States exported large amounts of gold in June and July 1928, and although it imported small amounts of gold over the remainder of the year, its cover ratio fell. France also saw its cover ratio decline during the second half of 1928; by November, it had fallen below 38 percent. As a result, the Bank of France began to convert dollars and pounds into gold, and its cover ratio began to rise, ending the year at 38.46 percent (Mouré 1991, 47–48).

The situation changed dramatically in early 1929. By May 1929, the United States and France were holding 5 percent of the world's gold stock in excess of that needed to maintain their 1928 cover ratio. This means that about 5 percent of the world's gold stock was effectively withdrawn from world circulation and demonetized. (That gold became inactivate in 1929 in the sense that it was more than what would have been required to maintain the 1928 cover ratio, given the actual outstanding liabilities in 1929.) Although the United States eased its policy by the end of the year, the two countries took an average of 3.5 percent of the world's gold stock out of the international financial system over the course of 1929—the United States about 2.1 percentage points and France about 1.4 percentage points (about a 60/40 percent breakdown).

By early 1930, the United States and France had taken 9.5 percent of the world's gold reserves out of the system, the United States accounting for 6 percentage points and France 3.5 percentage points (again about a 60/40 breakdown, which was maintained throughout this period). By the end of the year, France's cover ratio had risen to well over 50 percent. In January 1931, the Bank of France considered suspending gold purchases if the cover ratio were to hit 55 percent, which it soon did, but this idea was rejected on the grounds that such a move would require legislation and would risk an appreciation of the franc (Mouré 2002, 188).

When the European financial crisis struck in mid-1931, even more gold flowed to the United States and France. By August 1931, the United States and France held 12.6 percent of the world's gold stock in excess reserves (7.2 percentage points for the United States, 5.4 percent for France). However, the situation once again changed dramatically in late 1931 when Britain left the gold standard and gold rapidly fled the United States in fear that the dollar would be devalued. The U.S. cover ratio fell sharply while France's cover ratio reached 60 percent by the end of the year. By this point, the international gold standard had largely disintegrated.

In sum, the United States and France exerted roughly comparable pressure on foreign gold reserves in 1929, 1930, and through most of 1931, with the United States accounting for about 60 percent of the excess gold holdings to France's 40 percent. Figure 8 shows the path of the world's actual gold reserves, which were climbing steadily during this period, and the path of its "effective" gold reserves, which deducts the nonmonetized excess reserves of the United States and France. This latter path shows the sharp tightening of policy in early 1929 and again in early 1930. Rather than growing steadily, the effective amount of gold circulating in the world was flat in 1929, 1930, and 1931.

Figure 8
Actual and Effective World Gold Reserves, 1928–31

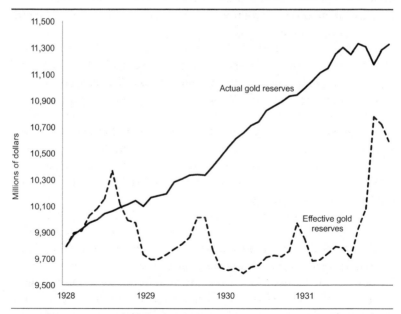

Source: Author's calculations. See text.

4. THE IMPACT OF EXCESSIVE GOLD HOLDINGS
ON WORLD PRICES

In his 1752 essay "Of Money," David Hume remarked, "If the coin be locked up in chests, it is the same thing with regard to prices, as if it were annihilated." This analogy is relevant to the American and French accumulation of gold during this period. How did the massive withholding of gold from the rest of the world by the United States and France, starting in early 1929, affect world prices?

Although wholesale prices had been stable in most countries in the mid- to late-1920s, a powerful deflationary shock struck countries simultaneously in mid-1929. The precise timing of this deflationary price shock is, not coincidentally, closely related to the changes in French and American monetary policies. As Figure 9 shows,

Figure 9
Monthly Wholesale Prices, 1926–32

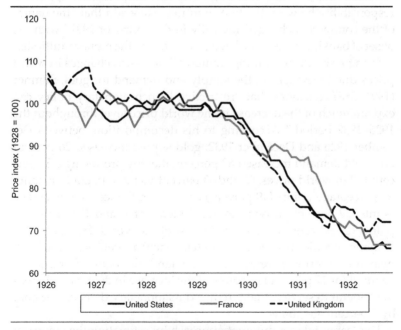

Source: League of Nations, *Statistical Yearbook of the League of Nations 1931/32,* various pages.

wholesale prices started falling in the summer of 1929 and did not stop until mid-1932, by which time many countries had left the gold standard. Prices fell about 5 percent in 1929, 15 percent in 1930, and another 14 percent in 1931, before stabilizing in 1932. This fall in prices was largely unanticipated (Hamilton 1992; Evans and Wachtel 1993). The onset of the Great Depression in terms of falling output and rising unemployment is largely coincidental with the sharp and synchronized decline in world prices starting in mid-1929.

Two studies have focused on the role of central banks in generating the deflation of the early 1930s. Bernanke and Mihov (2000) decompose national price movements resulting from changes in the money supply into components such as changes in the money multiplier, cover ratios, reserve-to-gold ratios, and the stock of gold. They conclude that the collapse in the world money supply was not due to a shortage of monetary gold. Rather, the monetary contraction in 1929 and 1930 resulted from the discretionary component of monetary policy, specifically the sterilization of gold by the United States and "to some extent" France, although they do not specifically apportion responsibility between the two countries. They add that "the nature of the contraction changed radically in the spring of 1931" with the onset of banking crises, which led to a decline in the money multiplier.

Using a simple accounting framework to assess changes in world prices due to changes in the supply and demand for gold, Sumner (1991, 388) concludes that "restrictive French monetary policy can explain much of the decrease in the world price level throughout the 1926–1932 period." According to his decomposition, between December 1926 and December 1932, gold supply increased 26 percent and gold demand increased 63 percent, thereby producing a 37 percent fall in world prices. Of the 63 percent increase in gold demand, 31 percentage points (49 percent) arose from France, 14 percentage points (22 percent) arose from the United States, and 17 percentage points (29 percent) arose from the rest of the world. However, this demand includes private demand (currency) as well as central bank demand. In terms of central bank demand, the Bank of France accounted for 17 percentage points of the increase in demand, whereas the Federal Reserve actually reduced its monetary demand for gold by 5 percentage points.

This paper takes a different approach by estimating the empirical relationship between the gold stock and world prices to see how much of the decline in prices can be attributed to the deviation between the actual and effective world gold stock. Barro (1979) presents a simple model of the gold standard that gives us a more formal framework in which we can interpret the impact of changes in gold supplies on world prices. Under the gold standard, the supply of money is assumed to be a constant multiple of the monetary gold stock:

$$(1) \qquad M_S = \lambda P_G G$$

where M_S is the money supply, P_G is the nominal price of gold, G is the stock of monetary gold, and λ is a multiplier that relates currency and demand deposits to the value of the monetary gold stock. Money demand is assumed to take the form

$$(2) \qquad M_D = kPY$$

where M_D is money demand, P is the price level, Y is the level of real output, and k is the ratio of money demand to income. The nominal price of gold—P_G—is fixed under the gold standard, and λ is assumed to be constant. This implies the following:

$$(3) \qquad \Delta \log P_t = \Delta \log G_t - \Delta \log k_t - \Delta \log Y_t$$

Unfortunately, because of insufficient data, any changes in the ratio of money demand to income over time (k) becomes part of the error term. Therefore, the empirical specification is

$$(4) \qquad \Delta \log P_t = \alpha + \beta \, \Delta \log G_t + \mu \, \Delta \log Y_t + \varepsilon_t$$

This specification assumes that G is exogenous. Although there is no allowance for the possibility that a lower price level (i.e., a higher relative price of gold) could lead to an increase in the production of gold, historical evidence strongly suggests that this is an appropriate assumption. It is commonly accepted that gold production was inelastic in the short run, that is, with respect to year-to-year price fluctuations.[21] Even over the longer run, Rockoff (1984) and Eichengreen and McLean (1994) find that changes in gold supply prior to 1913 were determined by new discoveries and factors other than the price of gold.

---

[21] As Sumner (1991, 383) notes, "changes in the supply of monetary gold could only slightly reduce the impact of changes in gold-reserve ratios on the price level, at least in the short- to medium-term."

The coefficients of this equation have an economic interpretation. The constant term can be interpreted as the change in the price level without any growth in the supply of gold. Cassel (1928), Kitchen (1930), and others all emphasized how world commodity prices were influenced by changes in the world gold stock and concluded that the world monetary stock of gold would have to increase about 3 percent per year to maintain stable world prices. If the monetary stock rose at a slower rate, prices would fall; if the stock rose at a more rapid rate, prices would rise. This 3 percent factor reflected growing transactions and other demand for gold holdings. These economists showed this empirical regularity with an abundance of charts and tables (no regression analysis) depicting the world gold stock and a measure of world commodity prices back to the 1840s. Thus, we would expect the estimate of α to be about -0.03.

The coefficient β (the elasticity of the gold stock with respect to commodity prices) should be about 1, because a 10 percent increase in the world gold stock would increase the monetary base 10 percent and would likely increase prices 10 percent. We would expect the coefficient on income to be positive, but we would not have a strong prior opinion about its precise magnitude.

Annual data on the world monetary gold stock and wholesale price index are presented in League of Nations (1930a, 82–84).[22] Annual data on world income (real gross domestic product) for Western Europe and other offshoots (the United States, Canada, Australia, and New Zealand) come from Angus Maddison's database.[23]

The results from estimating equation (4) for the period of the classical gold standard (1870–1914) is

$$\Delta \log P_t = -0.04 + 0.87 \, \Delta \log G_t + 0.72 \, \Delta \log Y_t + \varepsilon_t$$
$$\quad\;\; (0.01) \;\; (0.45) \qquad\quad (0.27)$$

HAC standard errors are in parenthesis and the adjusted R^2 is 0.12. The Breusch-Gofrey serial correlation test ($F = 0.36$) rejects the hypothesis that the errors are serially correlated.

---

[22] The most frequently used measure of world prices was the Sauerbeck-Statist index, the longest available series of world commodity prices dating back to the early 19th century. The Sauerbeck-Statist index after 1929 comes from Mitchell (1988).

[23] Maddison's database can be found online at http://www.ggdc.net/MADDISON/Historical_Statistics/horizontal-file_02-2010.xls. Accessed November 14, 2010.

The estimate of the constant term is -0.04, which supports Cassel's contention that the demand for gold was growing at about 3 percent annually and therefore world gold supplies would need to expand at least that much to maintain the world price level. The coefficient on the change in the gold stock suggests that a 10 percent increase in world gold reserves would increase world prices by almost 9 percent; one cannot reject the hypothesis that the coefficient is 1.

The sample can be extended back to 1840 ($n = 74$) if one is willing to forgo the income term. The estimated relationship is

$$\Delta \log P_t = -0.03 + 0.92 \, \Delta \log G_t + \varepsilon_t$$
$$ (0.01) \quad (0.38)$$

HAC standard errors are in parenthesis and the adjusted R^2 is 0.10. The Breusch-Gofrey serial correlation test ($F = 0.92$) rejects the hypothesis that the errors are serially correlated.[24]

While these estimates give us some information about the relationship between changes in gold supplies and world prices, the relationship between gold and prices may have been very different in the post–World War I period. It is difficult to test whether this is the case due to the lack of annual observations of countries on the gold standard in the 1920s. Therefore, the prediction of how prices would have behaved in the absence of the U.S. and French gold accumulation depends on the pre–World War I relationship still holding. We cannot be completely assured that this is the case, but must presume so to do the calculation.

Figure 10 shows the close historical relationship between the change in world gold reserves and the change in world prices from 1840 to 1914 (using the second estimated equation). The gold standard was suspended during World War I and thereafter, so prices and gold became delinked. Prices rose sharply during the war and fell precipitously in 1921, both of which are accounted for with dummy variables for World War I (1915–17) and the postwar price decline (1921). The equation allows us to predict the further path of prices based on the actual change in the world's monetary gold stock.

---

[24] Barsky and De Long (1991) estimate a bivariate regression of wholesale price inflation on gold production but find a coefficient of 2.47 for the period 1880–1913. However, they note that the coefficient should be close to unity.

The monetary gold stock grew 14 percent between 1928 and 1932, a compound annual rate of 3.4 percent. Despite the concerns about an insufficient supply of gold, there was no apparent shortage of monetary gold during this period. However, this growth is very close to the constant term α, and as a result, world prices would be expected to be roughly stable over this four-year period. Of course, instead of remaining stable, world prices *fell* 34 percent between 1928 and 1932.

Figure 10 shows actual world prices from 1840 to 1933, predicted world prices from 1840 to 1925, and the out-of-sample forecast of prices from 1925 to 1933. This illustrates the powerful deflationary shock that hit during this period and how difficult it would have been to anticipate a significant price decline given the growing supply of gold during this period. For some reason, the growth in the world's monetary gold stock was not being translated into stable world

Figure 10
Actual and Predicted Wholesale Prices, 1840–1933

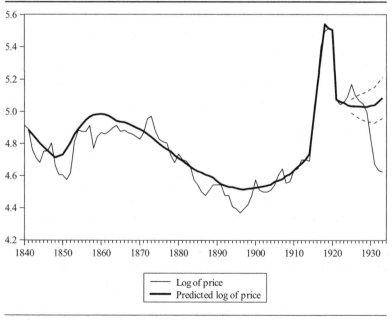

Source: See text, pp. 34–36.
Note: $+/-2$ standard errors included with the forecast price level.

Table 4
Actual and Expected Changes in Prices (Percent)

	Change in Gold Stock	Expected Change in Prices	Actual Change in Prices	Percent Change in Effective Gold Stock	Expected Change in Prices
1929	2.4	−0.8	−5.1	−4.8	−7.4
1930	3.4	0.1	−15.7	−1.7	−4.5
1931	2.7	−0.5	−14.4	0.5	−2.5

prices. The likely reason for this outcome was the effective reduction in the monetized gold stock due to U.S. and French actions.[25]

The results are summarized in Table 4. In 1929, the world gold stock grew 2.4 percent, not enough to prevent a potential small decline in prices of nearly 1 percent. But prices actually fell 5 percent because the United States and France effectively withdrew 5 percent of the world's gold stock from circulation in 1929. Given our estimate of the elasticity of prices with respect to the gold stock (about 0.9), world prices in 1929 would have been expected to fall 7 percent ($-4.8 \times 0.9 - 0.04$), other things being equal in that year. In 1930, the effective gold stock fell nearly 2 percent, suggesting that prices would have been expected to fall almost 5 percent, when in fact they fell almost 16 percent. In 1931, the effective gold stock was stable and so prices would have been expected to fall 3 percent, when in fact they fell 14 percent. The impact on prices in 1932 matters less because many countries had left the gold standard by that point. The link between gold and prices was increasingly being severed, and France could accumulate all the gold it wanted without significantly affecting world prices.

From this simple exercise, we can conclude that the nonmonetization of gold inflows by the United States and France accounted for nearly

---

[25] Mazumder and Wood (forthcoming) argue that the severe deflation was inevitable once countries decided to return to prewar parity following the suspension of the gold standard during World War I and the subsequent wartime inflation. As Figure 10 indicates, the world price level did fall back to its prewar level by 1933. However, this fall was not necessarily inevitable because two major players, Germany and France, did not return to prewar parity, other smaller countries were on the gold exchange standard, and the United States never really followed the gold standard anyway. Even if one accepts the deflation as inevitable, Mazumder and Wood cannot explain the timing of the fall in prices; the evidence presented here suggests that American and French gold policies in the late 1920s were closely related to the sudden drop in prices.

40 percent of the worldwide deflation experienced between 1929 and 1931. World wholesale prices fell 34 percent during this period, of which 14 percentage points can be explained by the reduction in the world's effective gold stock over that period. Of course, once the deflationary spiral began, other factors began to reinforce it. The most important factor was growing insolvency (due to debt-deflation problems identified by Irving Fisher), which contributed to bank failures, which in turn led to a reduction in the money multiplier as the currency-to-deposit ratio increased (Boughton and Wicker 1979). However, these endogenous responses cannot be considered as independent of the initial deflationary impulse, and therefore U.S. and French policies can be held indirectly responsible for some portion of the remaining part of the price decline.

An important question that has been left unanswered is the reason for the nonneutrality of money; that is, why this deflation was associated with declining output. While falling prices need not imply contracting output and higher unemployment, recent research has shown that the Great Depression of the 1930s is somewhat unique in that the two factors were closely linked (Atkeson and Kehoe 2004; Bordo, Lane, and Redish 2004).

5. CONCLUSION

The standard account of the onset of the Great Depression usually begins with the tightening of U.S. monetary policy in 1928. However, the rapid accumulation and effective neutralization of gold reserves by France deserves equal billing in the narrative. This paper provides a simple explanation for the sudden onset of worldwide deflation in mid-1929 in terms of changes in U.S. and French monetary policy around 1928. The impact of the gold accumulation by each of the two countries was almost equally significant in producing deflationary pressure from 1929 to 1931.

Sweden's Gustav Cassel was one of the few contemporary economists to recognize this situation as it was happening. In lectures at Oxford in 1932, Cassel looked back on the preceding few years and blamed the United States and France for the economic disaster. "The fact that the gold-receiving countries failed to use their increasing gold reserves for extending the effective supply of means of payment must be regarded as abnormal and, therefore, as an independent cause of the fall in prices at the side of the maldistribution of gold," Cassel (1932, 70–71) argued. "The breakdown of the Gold Standard was the result of a flagrant mismanagement of this monetary mechanism." He rejected the excuses given by French and American authorities for their failure to monetize the gold inflows: "The fact that France and the United States have drawn disproportionate quantities of gold to themselves is certainly very disquieting, but the defense that is offered for this behavior is still more appalling."[26]

Because of the close association of the deflation with the depression in economic output, taking action to avert deflation during this period would likely have changed the course of world history. One shudders to think of the historical ramifications of the policies pursued at this time. As Robert Mundell (2000, 331) has speculated, "Had the price of gold been raised in the late 1920's, or, alternatively, had the major central banks pursued policies of price stability instead of adhering to the gold standard, there would have been no Great Depression, no Nazi revolution, and no World War II."

REFERENCES

Accominotti, Olivier. 2009. "The Sterling Trap: Foreign Reserves Management at the Bank of France, 1928–1936." *European Review of Economic History* 13: 349–76.

Atkeson, Andrew, and Patrick J. Kehoe. 2004. "Deflation and Depression: Is There an Empirical Link?" *American Economic Review* 94: 99–103.

Balogh, Thomas. 1930. "The Import of Gold into France: An Analysis of the Technical Position." *Economic Journal* 40: 422–60.

Barro, Robert J. 1979. "Money and the Price Level under the Gold Standard." *Economic Journal* 89: 13–33.

Barsky, Robert B., and J. Bradford De Long. 1991. "Forecasting Pre–World War I Inflation: The Fisher Effect and the Gold Standard." *Quarterly Journal of Economics* 106: 815–36.

Bernanke, Ben. 1995. "The Macroeconomics of the Great Depression: A Comparative Approach." *Journal of Money, Credit, and Banking* 27: 1–28.

Bernanke, Ben, and Harold James. 1991. "The Gold Standard, Deflation, and Financial Crisis in the Great Depression: An International Comparison." In *Financial Markets and Financial Crises,* ed. R. Glenn Hubbard. Chicago: University of Chicago Press for the National Bureau of Economic Research.

Bernanke, Ben, and Ilian Mihov. 2000. "Deflation and Monetary Contraction in the Great Depression: An Analysis by Simple Ratios." In *Essays on the Great Depression,* ed. Ben Bernanke. Princeton, NJ.: Princeton University Press.

Board of Governors of the Federal Reserve System. 1943. *Banking and Monetary Statistics.* Washington, D.C.: Board of Governors of the Federal Reserve System.

---

[26] Also looking back on this period, Ralph Hawtrey (1932, 38) stated, "I am inclined therefore to say that while the French absorption of gold in the period from January 1929 to May 1931 was in fact one of the most powerful causes of the world depression, that is only because it was allowed to react to an unnecessary degree upon the monetary policy of other countries."

Bordo, Michael D., John Landon Lane, and Angela Redish. 2004. "Good versus Bad Deflation: Lessons from the Gold Standard Era." NBER Working Paper No. 10329.

Boughton, James M., and Elmus R. Wicker. 1979. "The Behavior of the Currency-Deposit Ratio during the Great Depression." *Journal of Money, Credit, and Banking* 11: 405–18.

Cassel, Gustav. 1928. *Postwar Monetary Stabilization*. New York: Columbia University Press.

———. 1930. "Pathways to Prosperity: The Slump in World Trade." *The Living Age* October: 118–20.

———. 1932. *The Crisis in the World's Monetary System*. Oxford: Clarendon Press.

Choudhri, Ehsan, and Levis Kochin. 1980. "The Exchange Rate and the International Transmission of Business Cycle Disturbances: Some Evidence from the Great Depression." *Journal of Money, Credit, and Banking* 12: 565–74.

Clarke, Stephen V. O. 1967. *Central Bank Cooperation, 1924–31*. New York: Federal Reserve Bank of New York.

Clavin, Patricia, and Jens-Wilhelm Wessels. 2004. "Another Golden Idol? The League of Nations' Gold Delegation and the Great Depression, 1929–32." *International History Review* 26: 765–95.

Eichengreen, Barry. 1986. "The Bank of France and the Sterilization of Gold, 1926–1932." *Explorations in Economic History* 23: 56–84.

———. 1990. *Elusive Stability: Essays in the History of International Finance, 1919–1939*. New York: Cambridge University Press.

———. 1992. *Golden Fetters: The Gold Standard and the Great Depression, 1919–1939*. New York: Oxford University Press.

Eichengreen, Barry, and Ian W. McLean. 1994. "The Supply of Gold under the Pre-1914 Gold Standard." *Economic History Review* 47: 288–309.

Eichengreen, Barry, and Jeffrey Sachs. 1985. "Exchange Rates and Economic Recovery in the 1930s." *Journal of Economic History* 45: 925–46.

Evans, Martin, and Paul Wachtel. 1993. "Were Price Changes during the Great Depression Anticipated? Evidence from Nominal Interest Rates." *Journal of Monetary Economics* 32: 3–34.

Friedman, Milton. 1991. "Forward" to Émile Moreau, *The Golden Franc: Memoirs of a Governor of the Bank of France: The Stabilization of the Franc (1926–1928)*, trans. Stephen D. Stoller and Trevor C. Roberts. Boulder, CO: Westview Press.

Friedman, Milton, and Anna J. Schwartz. 1963. *A Monetary History of the United States, 1867–1960*. Princeton, NJ: Princeton University Press.

Gardner, Walter R. 1932. "Central Bank Gold Reserves, 1926–1931." *American Economic Review* 22: 56–65.

Hamilton, James. 1987. "Monetary Factors in the Great Depression." *Journal of Monetary Economics* 19: 145–69.

———. 1988. "The Role of the International Gold Standard in Propagating the Great Depression." *Contemporary Policy Issues* 6 (2): 67–89.

———. 1992. "Was the Deflation during the Great Depression Anticipated? Evidence from the Commodity Futures Markets." *American Economic Review* 82: 157–78.

Hardy, Charles O. 1936. *Is There Enough Gold?* Washington, D.C.: Brookings Institution.

Hawtrey, Ralph. 1932. *The Art of Central Banking*. London: Longman, Green.

Irwin, Douglas A. 2011. "Anticipating the Great Depression? Gustav Cassel's Analysis of the Interwar Gold Standard." NBER Working Paper No. 17597. Forthcoming, *Journal of Money, Credit, and Banking*.

Johnson, H. Clark. 1997. *Gold, France, and the Great Depression, 1919–1932*. New Haven, CT: Yale University Press.

Keynes, John Maynard. 1929. "Is There Enough Gold? The League of Nations Inquiry." *The Nation and Athenaeum*, 19 January. In *Collected Works of John Maynard Keynes*, 19: 775–80.
———. 1932. *The World's Economic Crisis and the Way of Escape*. London: George Allen and Unwin.
———. 1981. *Collected Works of John Maynard Keynes*, Vol. 20. *Activities, 1929–31: Rethinking Employment and Unemployment Policies*. Cambridge: Cambridge University Press.
Kisch, C. H. 1931. "Memorandum on Legal Provisions Governing Reserves of Central Banks." In Royal Institute for International Affairs, *The International Gold Problem*. London: Oxford University Press.
Kitchin, Joseph. 1930. "Production and Consumption of Gold, Past and Prospective." In League of Nations (1930a).
League of Nations. 1930a. *Interim Report on the Gold Delegation of the Financial Committee*. Geneva: League of Nations.
Mazumder, Sandeep, and John H. Wood. Forthcoming. "The Great Deflation of 1929–33: It (Almost) Had to Happen." *Economic History Review*.
Mitchell, Brian R. 1988. *British Historical Statistics*. New York: Cambridge University Press.
Moggridge, Donald E. 1969. *The Return to Gold, 1925: The Formulation of Economic Policy and Its Critics*. Cambridge: Cambridge University Press.
Mouré, Kenneth. 1991. *Managing the Franc Poincaré: Economic Understanding and Political Constraint in French Monetary Policy, 1928–1936*. New York: Cambridge University Press.
———. 1996. "Undervaluing the Franc Poincaré." *Economic History Review* 49: 137–53.
———. 2002. *The Gold Standard Illusion: France, the Bank of France, and the International Gold Standard, 1914–1939*. New York: Oxford University Press.
Mundell, Robert A. 2000. "A Reconsideration of the Twentieth Century." *American Economic Review* 90: 327–40.
Nurkse, Ragnar. 1944. *The International Currency Experience: Lessons from the Interwar Period*. Geneva: League of Nations.
Patat, Jean-Pierre, and Michel Lutfalla. 1990. *A Monetary History of France in the Twentieth Century*. New York: St. Martin's.
Parker, Randall E. 2002. *Reflections on the Great Depression*. Northampton, MA: Edward Elgar.
Reynaud, Paul. 1933. "France and Gold." *Foreign Affairs* 11: 253–67.
Rist, Charles. 1932. "The International Consequences of the Present Distribution of Gold Holdings." In Royal Institute for International Affairs, *The International Gold Problem*. London: Oxford University Press.
Rockoff, Hugh. 1984. "Some Evidence on the Real Price of Gold, Its Costs of Production, and Commodity Prices." In *A Retrospective on the Classical Gold Standard, 1821–1931*, eds. Michael Bordo and Anna Schwartz. Chicago: University of Chicago Press.
Royal Institute for International Affairs. 1932. *The International Gold Problem*. London: Oxford University Press.
Sicsic, Pierre. 1992. "Was the Franc Poincaré Deliberately Undervalued?" *Explorations in Economic History* 29: 69–92.
———. 1993. "The Inflow of Gold to France from 1928 to 1934." *Notes d'Études et de Recherche*, Bank of France, No. 22.
Sumner, Scott. 1991. "The Equilibrium Approach to Discretionary Monetary Policy under an International Gold Standard, 1926–1932." *The Manchester School of Economic and Social Studies* 59: 378–94.
Temin, Peter. 1989. *Lessons from the Great Depression*. Cambridge, MA: MIT Press.

Comment

Charles W. Calomiris

Douglas Irwin's paper should encourage doctoral students in macroeconomics because it is one example of a broader phenomenon: the basic facts of some of the most important episodes of macroeconomic history remain obscure.

Irwin explores a key counterfactual question about the great deflation of the early 1930s. He shows that, absent the French monetary policies of that period, the great deflation would have been avoided, or at least greatly diminished. That is an important contribution; the failure of the gold standard to deliver a stable monetary regime in the interwar period was central to the history of the 20th century—not just to the monetary history of the 20th century—because without that failure, neither the Great Depression nor World War II would be imaginable. Economic historians, especially Barry Eichengreen, have been writing about the importance of the French absorption of gold in the late 1920s and early 1930s for a long time, and the conclusions Irwin reaches will not surprise them. But no one had quantified the extent of the French contribution to global deflation of the early 1930s.

Irwin's study is not just relevant for understanding the history of the Great Depression. It raises deep questions for international monetary policy today concerning the desirability of maintaining fixed exchange rate regimes. A central lesson of the French experience is that multilateral fixed exchange rate regimes like the gold standard are destined to end—and to produce catastrophic collapses when they do. Indeed, I would go further. That lesson also applies to the euro zone's currency union, even though its member countries have given up autonomous monetary policy (for now).

Charles W. Calomiris is the Henry Kaufman Professor of Financial Institutions at Columbia Business School, a research associate of the National Bureau of Economic Research, a member of the Shadow Open Market Committee, and a member of the Shadow Financial Regulatory Committee.

National politics are incompatible with an international monetary standard because national politics always trump international relations. International monetary standards, therefore, create monetary time bombs. Nations necessarily experience different economic shocks, and their political systems necessarily respond to those shocks *nationally*, balancing the relevant national political interests. International monetary agreements that seek to constrain those independent domestic responses are simply too weak. The euro zone sought to imitate the currency union of the United States, but that goal was founded on a political fantasy. The United States can maintain a currency union among its states because its currency union spans a nation, no less and no more. The world isn't a nation, and neither is Europe. When productivity growth differs among nations adhering to an international monetary standard (as it does in Greece and Germany today), the time bomb does not have a very long fuse. Even when two countries have more in common (like Germany and Spain), shocks that hit one but not the other will derail a currency union. Today's Spanish banking crisis is a prime example of such a shock.

From its beginnings, the international exchange rate system established after World War I was destabilizing because currency parities were established far from their equilibrium values. That created the need for substantial international balance-of-payments adjustments via gold flows, including substantial gold flows into France. That problem, however, could have been resolved through adjustments in income and prices (albeit painfully) without causing international havoc. The deeper problem that produced a global depression was that participating national governments, not market processes or global authorities, ultimately controlled how their nations adjusted to international gold flows. The countries importing huge amounts of gold (France and the United States) did not expand their money supplies enough to counter the deflationary pressures from the countries that were exporting gold and deflating their money supplied. The problem in the United States was largely that the Federal Reserve placed domestic objectives above international ones, although its conceptions about domestic monetary objectives were deeply flawed (Friedman and Schwartz 1963; Meltzer 2003; Calomiris 2012).

The problem in France was not just that central bankers failed to comprehend the importance of the global supply of money for determining prices under the gold standard. Nor was it that they failed to see the need for cooperation among central bankers. Political and economic constraints prevented the Bank of France from expanding the French money supply in tandem with France's expanding gold holdings. Domestic factors trumped the so-called rules of the game, with dramatic and unintended international consequences.

It is important to emphasize that French policy did not consciously produce a global deflation. As Eichengreen (1982; 1986) has shown, the French government and the Bank of France were constrained in their actions, and those constraints likely reflected a combination of factors, including prior French monetary and political history, and the condition of French banks. Furthermore, the nature of French economic expansion during the late 1920s—which was heavily focused on capital investment rather than export production—did not promote speedy automatic adjustment of the balance of payments in reaction to French gold inflows. Indeed, from 1926 to 1932, the French real exchange rate and real wages in tradable goods were quite stable.

The global economy, therefore, needed a forward-looking, activist French policy of monetary, credit, and fiscal expansion to make international adjustment work, but those policies were inconsistent with the actions of the Bank of France, the French government, and the French commercial banks. The central bank's "cover" reserve ratio rose consistently from 1928 to 1931, from 40 percent to 80 percent. Not only was high-powered money constrained by the lack of central bank actions, but the money multiplier was falling, mainly as the result of French banks' desire to accumulate reserves, as the French banks boosted their reserves-to-deposit ratio. And the French government ran substantial budget surpluses.

These actions were not the result of ignorance or stupidity; they were responses to the weakened institutional structure and heightened risks that plagued French public finances, central banking, and its commercial banks. Poincaré's ascendancy in 1926 was a big positive for French political and economic management, but it was not a miracle drug to instantly heal all of France's ailments (Eichengreen and Wyplosz 1986).

French budget surpluses were responding to the high risk of default on French public debt. At the end of World War I, France had a public debt-to-GDP ratio that reached nearly 200 percent. French budget deficits did not fall as quickly as those of Great Britain; from 1920 to 1923, they consistently ranged between 5 percent and 15 percent of GDP. The curtailment of reparation payments from Germany in 1924 contributed to widespread fears of rising tax burdens or high inflation. French sovereign yields remained substantially higher than British yields as late as 1927, although they fell below British yields in 1929 (Friedman 1953; Eichengreen 1982; Bordo and Hautcoeur 2003).

Most important, the Bank of France's latitude to pursue monetary expansion had been substantially circumscribed. In April 1925, the bank was implicated in a fraud involving public finances, which led to legislation that effectively prohibited the central bank from expanding the money supply (Eichengreen 1982; 1986). Commercial banks were also in a risky position, which led them to increase their reserve ratios as gold flowed into the country (Bouvier 1984).

In hindsight, France was in the middle of a sustainable expansion—one that left it much better off than Britain, Germany, and the United States by 1930. Hindsight, as they say, is "20/20." French fiscal, financial, and economic strength were all being tested in the 1920s, and they were not apparent until the Great Depression was underway. Economic adjustment in France took those domestic constraints into account; it had little choice to do otherwise. Furthermore, the political consequences of the central bank's involvement in fiscal fraud were (unsurprisingly) far-reaching and long-lived. When a central bank loses the trust of its nation, it should expect to be stripped of much of its discretionary authority. The timing of the Bank of France's emasculation, of course, couldn't have been worse from the standpoint of the gold standard and the global economy.

What lessons can we derive from France's experience? The French gold sink reflected a "perfect storm" of economic and political circumstances, which produced a disastrous accumulation of gold, tight monetary policy, tight bank lending policy, and tight fiscal policy. The more important lesson, however, is that the reasons such storms happen have not disappeared. Nations, then and now, inevitably get into trouble, inevitably experience shocks that weaken their financial, fiscal, and monetary institutions, and inevitably handle those challenges more poorly than we economists would like since problems are addressed by imperfect political systems. The overarching lesson of France in the 1920s is that international monetary arrangements need to take all those facts seriously, rather than design exchange rate policies on the basis of ignorant, utopian fantasies. Of course, expecting countries to behave that way would itself be an ignorant, utopian fantasy. The apparent impossibility of learning in international monetary affairs ensures that monetary history will remain an interesting subject.

REFERENCES

Bouvier, Jean. 1984. "The French Banks, Inflation and the Economic Crisis, 1919–1939." *Journal of European Economic History* 13 (Fall): 29–80.

Bordo, Michael D., and Pierre-Cyrille Hautcoeur. 2003. "Why Didn't France Follow the British Stabilization after World War One?" NBER Working Paper No. 9860.

Calomiris, Charles W. 2012. "Volatile Times and Persistent Conceptual Errors: U.S. Monetary Policy, 1914–1951." In *The Origins, History and Future of the Federal Reserve.* Atlanta: Federal Reserve Bank of Atlanta.

Eichengreen, Barry. 1982. "Did Speculation Destabilize the French Franc in the 1920s?" *Explorations in Economic History* 19: 71–100.

Eichengreen, Barry. 1986. "The Bank of France and the Sterilization of Gold, 1926–1932." *Explorations in Economic History* 23: 56–84.

Eichengreen, Barry, and Charles Wyplosz. 1986. "The Economic Consequences of the Franc Poincaré." NBER Working Paper No. 2064.

Friedman, Milton. 1953. *Essays in Positive Economics.* Chicago: University of Chicago Press.

Friedman, Milton, and Anna J. Schwartz. 1963. *A Monetary History of the United States, 1867–1960.* Princeton, NJ: Princeton University Press.

Meltzer, Allan H. 2003. *A History of the Federal Reserve, 1913–1951.* Chicago: University of Chicago Press.

Comment

James D. Hamilton

Douglas Irwin has provided a useful investigation into what went wrong during the world's brief return to an international gold standard in the late 1920s. He has uncovered some prescient historical analysis from Keynes and others and provides useful new analysis that lays the blame on both France and the United States for trying to accumulate too much of the world's gold stock between 1928 and 1931.

Some insight into what happened can be gained by considering an economy in which there is only a single produced good, which for concreteness I will call a "potato." The aggregate price level for this economy, P, is simply the number of dollars it would cost to buy a potato. The relative price of gold, R, is the number of potatoes it would cost to buy an ounce of gold. We then have the accounting identity that the number of dollars needed to obtain an ounce of gold is given by

$$(1) \qquad \frac{P \text{ dollars}}{\text{potato}} \times \frac{R \text{ potatoes}}{\text{ounce of gold}} = PR \frac{\text{dollars}}{\text{ounce of gold}}.$$

Now, if by a gold standard we mean a system in which the number of dollars necessary to obtain an ounce of gold (PR) is fixed, then a decrease in the aggregate price level P and an increase in the relative price of gold R are one and the same thing. In thinking about why countries on the gold standard—such as the United States, France, and Britain—experienced broad deflation between 1929 and 1931, we can equally well ask what factors gave rise to an increase in the relative price of gold over this period.

James D. Hamilton is professor of economics at the University of California, San Diego.

Irwin's Figure 1 provides one way to frame this question. If we think of the relative price of gold (R in my notation) as the value that equates gold supply with gold demand, then an event that increased the demand for gold would, for countries adhering to the gold standard, require deflation in overall money prices.

Irwin's empirical support for the claim that this is what happened is based on the amount by which France and the United States increased their holdings of gold relative to notes in circulation and demand deposits after 1928. Although the evidence is consistent with Irwin's hypothesis, it's not a necessary ingredient. Returning to the logic of Irwin's Figure 1, suppose that France and the United States had been the only two countries in the world, that the two countries were identical in all respects, and that both countries wanted to increase their gold holdings at the same time. Their respective central banks could raise interest rates to attract gold inflows but of course could not produce any new gold for the system. Instead, raising rates would have the effect of reducing domestic demand and, insofar as this depressed the domestic price level P, would correspond under a gold standard to an increase in the relative price of gold R. The logic of Figure 1 clearly implies that P can change without any change in the physical stocks of gold held by any central bank.

Thus we should look not just at the ex post results of which countries ended up acquiring additional gold, but also at the underlying forces that may have induced France and possibly other central banks and private citizens to want to accumulate more gold in the first place. Answering that question necessitates commenting on the experience with inflation in Europe in the years before Irwin's analysis begins.

In my Figure 1, I have plotted the price levels of France, the United Kingdom, and the United States over the three years before Irwin's Figure 9 begins: 1923–26. Although prices in the UK and the United States had been steady, France at that time was not on the gold standard and saw domestic prices double over the three-year period. In this, the country was not alone. Belgium's experience (also shown in Figure 1) was similar. Germany's hyperinflation earlier in the decade is quite famous. The 1920s also saw slightly less spectacular hyperinflations in Austria, Hungary, Poland, and Russia. This experience was what led France (along with 30 other countries that had been

Figure 1
Wholesale Prices across Countries, 1923–26

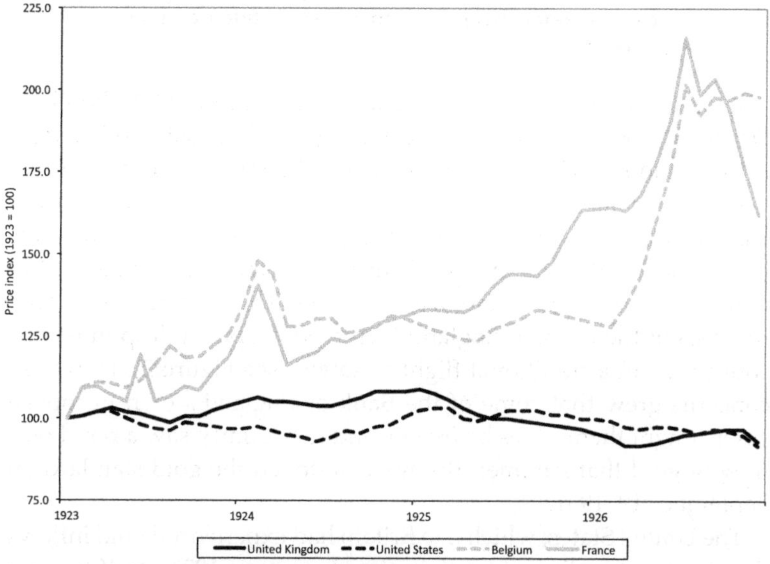

Source: *League of Nations Statistical Yearbook* (1926), available online at http://digital.
library.northwestern.edu/league/stat.html.
Notes: Wholesale price level (Jan. 1923 = 100) for Belgium, France, United Kingdom,
and United States, monthly, Jan. 1923 to Dec. 1926.

off gold) to try to return to the gold standard in the late 1920s. As
Eichengreen and Temin (2000, 198) observed,

> France had suffered a socially divisive inflation in the first half
> of the twenties, when gold convertibility was in abeyance.
> The budget had run out of control until the government again
> was subjected to gold-standard discipline. Commentators
> came away convinced that disregard for the gold standard
> led to financial excesses, economic chaos and social turmoil.

And Cooper (1992, 2126–27) noted that the instability of the 1920s
continued to constrain the Bank of France through the early 1930s:

> It is worth noting, however, that from late 1930 the French
> public, having disgorged gold on a substantial scale dur-

ing the late 1920s, began to acquire gold on a massive scale throughout 1931–33, even while the Bank of France was acquiring gold. Thus the Bank was reminded of the possibility, indeed the likelihood, that the French public was a potential source of major conversion if they lost confidence in the national currency.

If economic recovery had begun at the end of 1930, the Great Depression would likely have been regarded as just another typical recession. I will therefore focus on the strains on the international financial system in 1931. The failure of Credit-Anstalt, Austria's biggest bank, in May 1931, was followed by bank runs in Czechoslovakia, Germany, Hungary, Poland, and Romania. Initially, following these—and in a traditional flight to safety—the gold reserves of the Bank of England increased despite a drop in its discount rate, in a traditional flight to safety (see Figure 2). However, concerns grew that some of the Bank of England's own European assets might themselves be frozen, and the country saw a rapid outflow of gold that summer. Britain abandoned the gold standard on September 19, 1931.

The United States, which like Britain had experienced gold inflows despite a lower discount rate in the summer of 1931, itself became the object of intense outflows after Britain had left the gold standard, under speculation that the U.S. dollar would be the next to suspend convertibility into gold (see Figure 3). The Federal Reserve entered the episode with six times as much gold as the Bank of England, and this, along with the stiff hike in U.S. interest rates, proved sufficient to end the speculative conversion of dollars to gold.

Although the United States and France managed to stay on the gold standard, the deflation they experienced was highly disruptive. Note that, for most countries, the economic recovery began when the country went off gold and thereby stopped the decline in the domestic price level P (see Figure 4).

This episode illustrates that the gold standard cannot by itself correct for an earlier lack of monetary and fiscal discipline. As I observed in Hamilton (1988, 87),

> A government lacking discipline in monetary and fiscal policy in the absence of a gold standard likely also lacks the discipline and credibility necessary for successfully adhering to a gold standard. Substantial uncertainty about the future

Figure 2
Bank of England Gold Reserves and Discount Rate, 1931

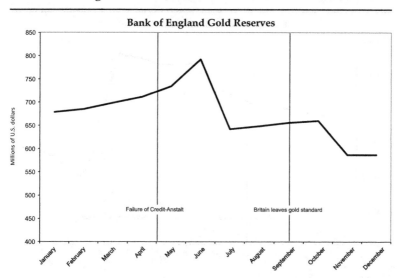

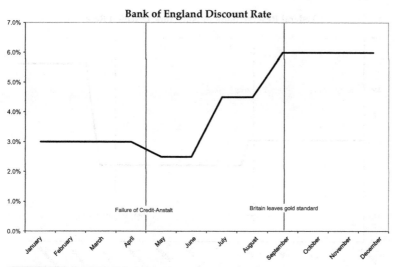

Sources: Top panel: Board of Governors of the Federal Reserve (1943, 551); Bottom panel: Global Financial Data, http://www.globalfinancialdata.com.
Note: Both panels show end-of-month values.

Figure 3
Federal Reserve Gold Reserves and Discount Rate, 1931

Federal Reserve Bank Gold Reserves

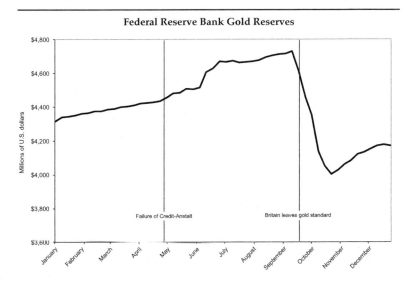

Federal Reserve Bank of New York Discount Rate

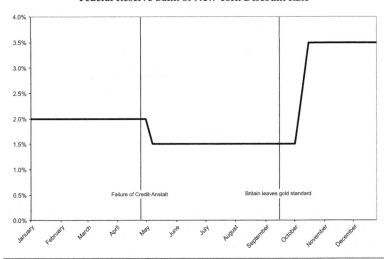

Sources: Top panel: Board of Governors of the Federal Reserve (1943, 385–86); Bottom panel: Board of Governors of the Federal Reserve (1943, 441).
Note: Weekly data.

Figure 4
Industrial Production for Countries Going Off the Gold Standard

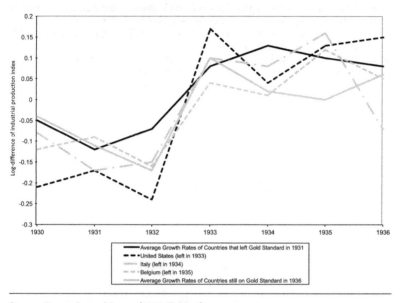

Source: Bernanke and James (1991, Table 4).

inevitably will result as speculators anticipate changes in the terms of gold convertibility. This institutionalizes a system susceptible to large and sudden inflows or outflows of capital and to destabilizing monetary policy if authorities must resort to great extremes to reestablish credibility. Such a system requires individuals to adapt their behavior to the contingencies of rapid and dramatic changes in interest rates, credit availability, and price levels. This characterizes the events of 1931 most accurately. Surely, it contributed to propagating the Great Depression.

Irwin's paper provides a good reminder of why an attempt to return to an international gold standard in 2013 would only be the beginning of our problems.

REFERENCES

Bernanke, Ben, and Harold James. 1991. "The Gold Standard, Deflation, and Financial Crisis in the Great Depression: An International Comparison." In *Financial Markets and Financial Crises*, ed. R. Glenn Hubbard. Chicago: University of Chicago Press for the National Bureau of Economic Research.

Board of Governors of the Federal Reserve. 1943. *Banking and Monetary Statistics: 1914–1941*. Washington, D.C.: Board of Governors of the Federal Reserve.

Cooper, Richard N. 1992. "Fettered to Gold? Economic Policy in the Interwar Period." *Journal of Economic Literature* 30: 2120–28.

Eichengreen, Barry, and Peter Temin. 2000. "The Gold Standard and the Great Depression." *Contemporary European History* 9: 183–207.

Hamilton, James D. 1988. "The Role of the International Gold Standard in Propagating the Great Depression." *Contemporary Policy Issues* 6 (2): 67–89.

An Empirical Analysis of the Fed's Term Auction Facility

Efraim Benmelech

ABSTRACT

The U.S. Federal Reserve used the Term Auction Facility to provide term funding to eligible depository institutions from December 2007 to March 2010. According to the Fed, the purpose of the TAF was to inject term funds through a broader range of counterparties and against a broader range of collateral than open market operations. The overall goal of the TAF was to ensure that liquidity provisions could be disseminated efficiently even when the unsecured interbank markets were under stress. In this paper, I use the TAF micro-level loan data and find that about 60 percent of TAF loans went to foreign banks that pledged asset-backed securities as collateral for these loans. The data and analysis illustrate the major role that foreign—in particular, European—banks currently play in the U.S. financial system and the resultant currency mismatch in their balance sheets. The data suggest that foreign banks had to borrow from the Federal Reserve Bank to meet their dollar-denominated liabilities.

Efraim Benmelech is an associate professor of finance in the Kellogg School of Management at Northwestern University and a research associate of the National Bureau of Economic Research.

I thank Ian Dew-Becker, Charlie Calomiris, Simon Gilchrist, James Hamilton, Laura Jones Dooley, Ross Levine, Jeff Miron, and seminar participants at the Cato Papers on Public Policy *Conference for useful comments. I acknowledge financial support from the Cato Institute. All errors are my own.*

An Empirical Analysis of the Fed's Term Auction Facility

1. INTRODUCTION

The Term Auction Facility program was one of the main tools used by the Federal Reserve and U.S. fiscal authorities during the recent financial crisis. The goal of this program, as described by the Federal Reserve, was to intervene in the interbank money markets in response to the difficulties experienced by banks in the United States and Europe. Initially, the Federal Reserve used open market operations to maintain the effective federal funds rate near its target rate and enacted several measures to encourage borrowing at the discount window.[1] However, these moves failed to stimulate the market as much as the Fed had expected. On December 12, 2007, therefore, the Federal Reserve introduced the TAF. The TAF provided longer-term financing to eligible depository institutions through auctions at predetermined dates. At its peak, the TAF amounted to more than $500 billion and was the largest expansion on the Federal Reserve's balance sheet. Lending through the TAF gradually faded away, and the final TAF auction was conducted on March 8, 2010.

One of the reasons for the introduction of the TAF during the early stages of the financial crisis was to provide banks with Federal Reserve liquidity without forcing them to face the stigma of borrowing from the discount window. Indeed, according to Federal Reserve Board Chairman Ben Bernanke, the associated stigma made banks reluctant to use the discount window:

> In August 2007, . . . banks were reluctant to rely on discount window credit to address their funding needs. The banks' concern was that their recourse to the discount window, if it became known, might lead market participants to infer weakness—the so-called stigma problem. (Bernanke 2009)

---

[1] To encourage banks to borrow at the discount window, the Federal Reserve reduced the discount window penalty rate from 100 basis points to 50 basis points on August 17, 2007, and extended the term of financing from overnight to as long as 30 days.

However, even borrowing from the TAF had a stigma attached to it. As a result, data on the loans that were made under the TAF, as well as the identity of the banks that participated in the auctions, were not disclosed initially. Later, the Federal Reserve disclosed data on the loans made under the TAF, as well as information on the other credit and liquidity programs it used during the crisis.

While the effectiveness of the TAF in reducing rates in the interbank market has been debated by both academic economists and policymakers (see, e.g., McAndrews, Sarkar, and Wang 2008 and Taylor and Williams 2009), little is known about the identity of the banks that participated in the auctions, the nature of the collateral used, or the terms of the individual loans. This paper fills in that gap by using the micro-level loan dataset released by the Federal Reserve. The TAF data, which contain detailed information on the loans and the participating financial institutions, provide a rare glimpse into the injection of emergency liquidity by the Federal Reserve as well as the identity of the banks obtaining credit and, in particular, the type of assets they pledged as collateral.

I found that foreign banks accounted for 58 percent of TAF lending, with a total amount of $2.2 trillion, compared to $1.6 trillion for U.S. banks. During the auction of December 2007 and through most of 2008, foreign banks accounted for the vast majority of the lending, with amounts that ranged between twofold and fourfold the total lending to U.S. banks. United Kingdom–based Barclays was the largest borrower in the TAF, followed by Bank of America, Royal Bank of Scotland, Wells Fargo, and Wachovia. Out of the 10 largest borrowers, five are foreign banks; out of the 50 largest borrowers, 33 are from foreign countries.

Next, I compared the collateral structure of domestic and foreign banks. I found that most of the banks and financial institutions that pledged asset-backed securities (ABSs) as collateral were foreign— primarily European—banks. For example, the bank that pledged the largest amount of ABSs for a given loan was Société Générale (France), followed by Norinchukin Bank (Japan), Dexia (Belgium), Barclays (UK), and UBS (Switzerland). Among the 10 banks that pledged the largest amounts of collateral, only two were American banks (State Street and U.S. Central Federal Credit Union). Why did the Federal Reserve allocate the majority of TAF loans to foreign banks? Why were foreign banks more likely to pledge the riskier ABSs and collateralized debt obligations (CDOs) as collateral?

One potential explanation is that the meltdown of the structured finance market and the severe deterioration in the credit ratings of ABSs necessitated liquidity injections to institutions that suffered major losses because of their exposure to the structured finance market. However, U.S. banks that borrowed from the TAF and had large exposures to ABSs, such as Citibank and Bank of America, did not pledge ABSs at the same level as European banks. Thus, while some of the Federal Reserve lending was probably aimed at injecting liquidity into financial institutions that held securities that were illiquid at the time, this is unlikely to be the only reason for the dominance of European banks in the TAF.

Another explanation for the large number of loans made to foreign banks is that these banks suffered from a currency mismatch in their balance sheets. Many foreign banks were active players in the creation and issuance of structured finance products. As money markets ground to a halt, those banks required financing to roll over their short-term liabilities. Furthermore, foreign banks were subject to a currency mismatch in their assets and liabilities. The main source of funding for some of the banks was demand deposits and other forms of credit in their home countries, and these were denominated in their home currencies (mostly the British pound and the euro). However, many European banks issued liabilities in U.S. money markets that were denominated in the U.S. dollar. Thus, not only were foreign banks subject to roll-over risk, they also suffered from a currency mismatch and had to rely on special facilities such as the currency swap lines between central banks (e.g., the European Central Bank, Bank of England, Swiss National Bank, and Federal Reserve), as well as on special lending programs such as the TAF. European banks were more likely to bid for TAF money because they were more severely affected by the financial crisis, given their exposure to a currency mismatch between assets and liabilities.

The rest of this paper is organized as follows: Section 2 provides the institutional details of the TAF. Section 3 describes the dataset and provides summary statistics on the evolution of the TAF over time. Section 4 displays the empirical analysis. Section 5 discusses the Federal Reserve's lending to foreign banks. Section 6 concludes.

61

2. THE TERM AUCTION FACILITY

Global money markets suffered serious disruptions in the summer of 2007 when the rates of interbank term loans rose to unusually high levels.[2] The TED spread—the difference between the three-month London interbank offered rate (LIBOR) and the three-month U.S. Treasury bill—rose from its typical level of 30 basis points to about 50 basis points and then to 200 basis points by the summer of 2007. This widening was a reason for major concern because the TED spread is an indicator of perceived credit risk in the general economy. Moreover, according to a New York Federal Reserve Bank research paper:

> [T]he volume of transactions in the inter-bank market declined, and borrowers reportedly often could not obtain funds at the posted rates. Since the LIBOR affects interest rates on a wide variety of loans and securities (e.g., home mortgages and corporate loans), unusually high term rates can have disruptive effects on the economy. (McAndrews, Sarkar, and Wang 2008, 1)

The Federal Reserve responded to the disruptions in the money markets with the traditional tool of monetary policy: open market operations to maintain the effective federal funds rate near its target rate. However, despite the Federal Reserve's efforts in the overnight funding market, the rates on term loans in the interbank market kept rising. In an attempt to ease the strains in the money markets, the Federal Reserve resorted to nontraditional tools of monetary policy. Perhaps the most important tool used for this purpose was the TAF.

The TAF was introduced on December 2007 in the early stages of the financial crisis to provide Federal Reserve liquidity funding by auctioning off short-term funding without forcing banks to face the stigma of borrowing from the Federal Reserve's discount window. Under the TAF, the Federal Reserve auctioned term funds to depository institutions. All depository institutions that were eligible to borrow under the primary credit program of the Federal Reserve were eligible to participate in TAF auctions. All loans extended under the TAF were fully collateralized. The funds were allocated through an auction in which participating depository institutions placed bids specifying an amount of funds, up to a pre-specified limit, and an

[2] Term funding is typically made with maturity terms of one month or longer.

interest rate that they would be willing to pay for such funds. The funds were allocated beginning with the highest interest rate offered until either all funds were allocated or all bids were satisfied. All borrowing institutions paid the same interest rate: either the rate associated with the bid that would fully subscribe the auction or, in the case that total bids were less than the amount of funds offered, the lowest rate that was bid. The TAF was created under the Federal Reserve's standard discount window lending authority granted under Section 10B of the Federal Reserve Act. The auctions were administered by the Federal Reserve Bank of New York, with loans granted through the 12 Federal Reserve banks.

TAF funding supplemented the U.S. dollar funding received by global banks around the world under the central bank swap facilities between the Federal Reserve banks and the Banco Central do Brasil, Bank of Canada, Denmark's Nationalbank, Bank of England, European Central Bank, Bank of Japan, Bank of Korea, Banco de Mexico, Reserve Bank of New Zealand, Norges Bank, Monetary Authority of Singapore, Sveriges Riksbank, and Swiss National Bank.

From the first TAF auction on December 17, 2007, to the last on March 8, 2010, the Federal Reserve conducted 60 auctions. The amount of term loans auctioned was initially between $20 billion and $30 billion, but was later increased to between $50 billion and $75 billion. The size increased to $150 billion in October 2008 and remained at that level until June 2009. During the second half of 2009 and the first three months of 2010, the amount auctioned gradually declined, and by the final auction in March 2010, only $3.4 billion was loaned out.

Whether the TAF was effective in reducing rates in the interbank market has been debated by both academic economists and policymakers. McAndrews, Sarkar, and Wang (2008) provide empirical evidence that the TAF has helped to ease strains in the interbank market. In contrast, according to Taylor and Williams (2009), the TAF had no impact on interest rate spreads. According to McAndrews, Sarkar, and Wang (2008), the major problem in the money markets in 2007–08 was lack of liquidity; hence the TAF was effective because it provided central bank liquidity to the banking system when the interbanking system collapsed. In contrast, Taylor and Williams (2009) argue that the main problem in the market was not liquidity but rather counterparty risk, which TAF funding could not have solved.

3. DATA AND SUMMARY STATISTICS

The data analyzed here come from Federal Reserve disclosure of each of the individual term loans provided under the TAF.[3] The dataset lists 4,214 individual loans spanning the auctions from December 12, 2007, to March 8, 2010.

The dataset includes micro-level detailed information for each loan contract on the contract terms, the borrower's identity, and the broad categories of the securities against which the loans were made. The loan contract terms include the interest rate on the loan (in percent), the loan maturity (in days), and the loan amount (in millions of dollars). The dataset also provides information on the borrower that includes the borrower's name, city, and state.[4] In addition, the Federal Reserve discloses information on the underlying collateral against which the loan was granted. In particular, it reports the amount of unencumbered collateral (defined as the lendable value of the borrower's collateral), as well as the broad categories of the assets used as collateral. The data comprise 12 asset-type categories: commercial loans, residential mortgages, commercial real estate loans, consumer loans, U.S. Treasury / Agency securities, municipal securities, corporate securities, mortgage-backed securities (MBSs) and collateralized mortgage obligations (CMOs) issued by government-sponsored enterprises, MBSs and CMOs issued by private corporations, ABSs, international securities, and other collateral. Finally, the dataset breaks down the dollar value of collateral by broad credit rating categories.

3.1 Loan Characteristics

Table 1 displays descriptive statistics for the main loan characteristics. The average loan amount (in millions) is $906.1 million, and the median is $125.0 million. The dispersion in loan amount ranges widely, from a minimum of $1.4 million (First Merchant Bank of Indiana) to the largest loans of $15 billion (to Bank of America, Barclays, Citibank, JP Morgan Chase, Wachovia, and Wells Fargo). The average loan term is 45.6 days and ranges from 13 days to 85 days. The average annualized interest rate is 0.900 percent and ranges from

---

[3] The data can be downloaded at http://www.federalreserve.gov/newsevents/reform_taf.htm#datadesc.

[4] For foreign borrowers, the dataset lists the city and state of their U.S. branch, which in most cases is New York City.

0.200 percent to 4.670 percent. As I explained in Section 2, the TAF was conducted through auctions in which all successful bids were subject to the same interest rate and loan terms. Thus, although loan amounts varied across banks and over time, all banks borrowing in the same auction obtained loans with the same interest rates and loan maturities.

In addition to the loan amount, there is strong heterogeneity in the amounts and types of collateral posted by the borrowing banks. Borrowers pledged unencumbered collateral with an average value of $4,285.4 million. Collateral values range from $5.1 million (Timberwood Bank) to $185,410.0 million (Bank of America); the median collateral value is $571.0 million. I also calculated the ratio of the face amount of the loan to the value of the unencumbered collateral and report it in the last row of Table 1. As the table shows, the average loan-to-collateral ratio is 0.334, and the median is 0.286. Loan-to-collateral rates increased after the peak of the crisis as collateral values increased and haircuts on collateral declined. For example, the average loan-to-value in 2008 was 0.255, compared to 0.370 and 0.460 in 2009 and 2010, respectively. Although the loan-to-collateral ratios appear to be low and conservative, it is not clear whether these numbers are based on market values or on face values of the underlying collateral.

3.2 The Collateral Structure of TAF Loans

Next I analyzed the composition of collateral in TAF loans. Given that loan terms as well as loan rates were determined at the auction level, the only sources of interbank variation were the amount of the loan and the amount and type of the collateral. Indeed, banks pledged different types of assets as collateral for their loans, and most TAF loans were secured by numerous securities from different asset types. Table 2 provides a detailed analysis of collateral structure for the 4,214 TAF loans. The table reports summary statistics for the dollar amount (in millions) as well as the number of loans for which collateral was pledged in each asset category.

The largest collateral category (based on the dollar amount of the assets pledged) is residential mortgages. The mean amount of residential mortgages used as collateral is $3,786.3 million, and it was used as collateral in 465 individual loans. The next largest category is ABSs, which according to the Federal Reserve definitions include

Table 1
Loan Characteristics

	Mean	25th Percentile	Median	75th Percentile	Standard Deviation	Minimum	Maximum	Observations
Loan amount (millions)	$906.1	$22.0	$125.0	$1,000.0	$1,922.5	$1.4	$15,000.0	4,214
Loan term (days)	45.6	28	28	84	25.6	13	85	4,214
Interest rate	0.900%	0.250%	0.250%	1.390%	1.093%	0.200%	4.670%	4,214
Collateral (millions)	$4,284.5	$79.3	$571.0	$4,157.9	$10,544.7	$5.1	$185,410.1	4,214
Loan-to-collateral ratio	0.334	0.150	0.286	0.477	0.227	0.004	1.001	4,214

Table 2
Collateral Composition by Security Type
(Millions, except observations)

	Mean	25th Percentile	Median	75th Percentile	Standard Deviation	Minimum	Maximum	Observations
Residential mortgages	$3,786.3	$7.9	$27.5	$402.9	$11,070.0	$0.0	$76,847.5	465
ABSs	$2,562.8	$91.5	$780.6	$2,513.4	$4,486.9	$0.4	$25,953.7	1,301
Commercial loans	$2,232.1	$40.1	$338.0	$1,544.4	$6,911.8	$0.1	$76,784.0	2,291
Consumer loans	$1,462.5	$8.8	$86.1	$1,194.1	$3,875.5	$0.0	$32,679.2	1,087
Private MBSs/CMOs	$1,154.9	$69.6	$241.7	$922.5	$2,378.8	$0.0	$14,599.2	1,045
Commercial real estate	$1,091.0	$35.9	$104.3	$718.9	$2,471.5	$0.0	$30,469.6	1,624
Corporate	$747.6	$43.6	$209.3	$1,115.9	$1,090.0	$0.1	$6,840.6	1,507
International securities	$703.1	$28.7	$129.7	$580.4	$1,492.0	$0.1	$11,302.5	1,138
Agency MBSs/CMOs	$567.9	$12.2	$80.2	$498.7	$1,681.2	$0.0	$26,679.8	1,151
Municipals	$370.3	$7.0	$20.1	$93.6	$1,180.6	$0.0	$8,911.9	1,099
U.S. Treasury/Agency	$348.8	$11.3	$48.5	$241.6	$968.7	$0.0	$8,762.4	833

securities collateralized by assets other than first-lien mortgages, including CDOs. More than 1,301 loans were backed by ABSs, and the mean collateral pledged in this category is $2,562.8 million and ranges from $0.4 million to $25,953.7 million.

The most popular asset class based on the number of loans that used it as collateral is commercial loans, which were used in 2,291 loans, followed by commercial real estate and corporate securities, which were used in 1,624 and 1,507 loans, respectively. Finally, U.S. Treasury / Agency securities were used in 833 loans, with a mean collateral value of $348.8 million.

The dataset also breaks down the collateral pool by credit rating categories.[5] Table 3 reports summary statistics for the collateral assets by the major credit rating classifications. AAA-rated U.S. Treasury / Agency securities (including agency MBSs and CMOs) amounted, on average, to $650.3 million. The amount of other AAA-rated securities pledged as collateral was on average $1,845.8 million per loan, and these were used in 1,859 loans. AA-rated and A-rated securities were used in 1,681 and 1,817 loans, respectively, and accounted for about $380 million each of the collateral pool. Other rating categories include BBB-rated (mean $238.0 million) and "other investment grade" securities (mean $1,232.6 million).

4. EMPIRICAL ANALYSIS

4.1 Determinants of Loan Characteristics

I began the empirical analysis of TAF loans by analyzing the characteristics of the loans. The eight ordinary least-squares regressions reported in Table 4 use different specifications to predict the determinants of the loan terms. For each of the four loan determinants, I report results from regressions that do not include bank fixed-effects (between analysis) and regressions that utilize variation over time using bank fixed-effects (within analysis). As explanatory variables, I used collateral dummy variables that take the value of "1" if a particular asset is included in the collateral pool and "0" otherwise. All regressions include year × month fixed-effects to account for time-varying effects.[6]

---

[5] The dataset reports asset types and credit ratings separately and hence does not enable classification that is based on both credit ratings and asset class.

[6] Although I used collateral dummy variables, the analysis yields similar results when using the actual share of collateral in each asset category.

Table 3
Collateral Composition by Credit Rating
(Millions, except observations)

	Mean	25th Percentile	Median	75th Percentile	Standard Deviation	Minimum	Maximum	Observations
AAA-rated								
U.S. Treasury / Agency and Agency MBSs-CMOs	$650.3	$13.4	$106.1	$555.8	$1,709.2	$0.0	$26,679.8	1,375
Other AAA-rated	$1,845.8	$22.2	$352.9	$1,801.7	$3,532.8	$0.0	$22,364.7	1,859
AA-rated	$381.6	$7.9	$74.2	$370.9	$857.8	$0.0	$8,505.2	1,681
A-rated	$386.5	$13.3	$96.3	$420.8	$783.3	$0.1	$7,775.7	1,817
BBB-rated	$238.0	$12.2	$68.5	$296.8	$422.9	$0.1	$4,881.4	1,694
Other investment-grade	$1,232.6	$42.3	$295.7	$1,088.1	$2,714.3	$0.0	$22,726.2	1,417

The table reports results for the following loan characteristics: loan amount (in logs), interest rate, loan term, and loan-to-collateral ratio. However, it should be noted that because TAF loans were granted at auction, the same interest rate and loan term applied to all banks participating in each auction. In contrast, the loan amount, the ratio of loan to collateral (the inverse of the loan "haircut"), and the nature of the assets pledged as collateral varied across banks within an auction. As Table 4 shows, the composition of the collateral has little explanatory power in bearing on loan outcomes. First, few if any of the explanatory variables turn out to be significant in regressions that use the interest rate or loan term as dependent variables. Second, the R-squared in the regressions shows that the addition of bank fixed-effects does not change the adjusted R-squared in the interest rate and loan term regressions, indicating that bank-specific effects had no impact on the loan rate and maturity.[7]

In contrast, collateral composition significantly affected both loan amount and loan-to-collateral ratio. As the first column shows, ABSs, commercial real estate, international securities, Treasuries, private MBSs, and consumer loans are associated with larger loans, whereas municipal securities are correlated with smaller loans. However, given that the regressions do not control for bank characteristics, it is likely that some of the collateral results are driven by omitted variables. For example, if larger banks are more likely to hold ABSs or international bonds, then the positive coefficient in column one might be capturing the simple correlation between bank size and loan amount. In an attempt to address this concern, the regression specification reported in column two adds bank fixed-effects to the analysis and hence uses variation within a bank from repeated loans in several TAF auctions over time. Indeed, as the second column of the table demonstrates, only commercial real estate, Treasury, and private MBSs survive the addition of fixed-effects and are still positive and significant. In addition, residential mortgages and corporate bonds turn out to be positive and significant when fixed-effects are added.

Turning to the last two columns of the table, I find that loans secured by ABSs obtained loan-to-collateral ratios between

---

[7] The high R-squared in the interest rate is completely driven by the year × month fixed-effects since there was an overall trend of declining interest rates throughout the TAF time period.

Table 4
Determinants of Loan Terms

	Log (loan amount)		Interest Rate		Loan Term		Loan-to-Collateral	
	Between	Within	Between	Within	Between	Within	Between	Within
ABS dummy	1.570***	−0.001	0.008	−0.016	0.444	0.544	−0.150***	−0.052***
	(0.084)	(0.088)	(0.006)	(0.020)	(1.152)	(2.708)	(0.010)	(0.019)
Commercial real estate dummy	0.446***	0.220***	−0.004	−0.010	−1.079	−0.680	−0.069	−0.034
	(0.061)	(0.068)	(0.004)	(0.009)	(0.813)	(1.859)	(0.007)	(0.014)
International dummy	0.850***	0.047	−0.007	−0.008	2.417**	−0.775	0.004	−0.005
	(0.082)	(0.069)	(0.007)	(0.014)	(1.122)	(1.967)	(0.011)	(0.016)
Municipal dummy	−0.242***	−0.017	0.002	0.017	−1.396	−2.951*	0.011	−0.022
	(0.059)	(0.059)	(0.004)	(0.011)	(0.899)	(1.762)	(0.008)	(0.014)
Treasury dummy	0.279***	0.217***	−0.004	−0.005	−1.170	−2.762	0.051***	0.030**
	(0.059)	(0.062)	(0.005)	(0.010)	(0.998)	(1.899)	(0.009)	(0.014)
Private MBS dummy	−0.067 / 0.881***	0.275***	0.001	−0.017	−0.214	−1.899	−.045***	−0.019
	(0.087)	(0.086)	(0.010)	(0.016)	(1.152)	(2.268)	(0.010)	(0.016)
Agency dummy	0.046	0.048	−0.003	−0.008	0.088	−3.398**	0.004	0.002
	(0.062)	(0.057)	(0.004)	(0.009)	(0.960)	(1.673)	(0.009)	(0.013)

(continued)

Table 4
(continued)

	Log (loan amount)		Interest Rate		Loan Term		Loan-to-Collateral	
	Between	Within	Between	Within	Between	Within	Between	Within
Residential mortgage dummy	0.035	0.324***	-0.000	0.024	-6.267***	-7.223***	0.052***	-0.037*
	(0.095)	(0.108)	(0.005)	(0.020)	(1.105)	(2.549)	(0.012)	(0.022)
Consumer loans dummy	0.454***	0.203**	-0.003	-0.005	0.959	-4.037*	-0.073***	-0.063***
	(0.070)	(0.103)	(0.004)	(0.017)	(0.865)	(2.401)	(0.008)	(0.020)
Corporate securities dummy	0.111	0.340***	0.007	0.007	-1.613	1.740	0.047***	-0.034*
	(0.077)	(0.082)	(0.006)	(0.015)	(1.091)	(2.192)	(0.011)	(0.020)
Fixed-effects								
Year × Month	Yes	Yes	Yes	Yes	Yes	Yes	Yes	Yes
Bank	No	Yes	No	Yes	No	Yes	No	Yes
Pseudo/Adjusted R^2	0.41	0.93	0.99	0.99	0.39	0.39	0.19	0.59
Observations	4,214	4,214	4,214	4,214	4,214	4,214	4,214	4,214

Note: Omitted collateral category is commercial loans. * = 10% significance level; ** = 5% significance level; *** = 1% significance level. Standard errors in parentheses.

−0.150 and −0.052 lower. Likewise, consumer loans led to lower loan-to-value ratios, while loans secured by Treasuries had loan-to-collateral ratios that were higher by 0.030. The results are consistent with the notion that haircuts on collateral are an important tool for monetary policy. This is important especially when nontraditional monetary policy is conducted through auctions in which the interest rate and loan terms do not vary across borrowers.

4.2 The Evolution of TAF over Time

Figure 1 displays the evolution of the TAF lending facility size over time. As described in Section 2, the Federal Reserve announced the offering amount in advance of each auction. As Figure 1 shows, the initial auctions were smaller, with amounts between $20 and $30 billion. The offering amount was raised to $50 billion in the March 10, 2008, auction and was further increased to $75 billion on May 5, 2008. While the amounts fluctuated between $25 billion and $75 billion in August and September 2008, the lending facilities increased dramatically to $150 billion on October 6, 2008, during the peak of the financial crisis, and remained at that level until the end

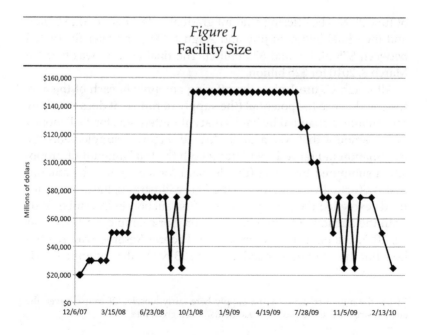

Figure 1
Facility Size

Figure 2
Total Proposition Submitted and Amount Awarded

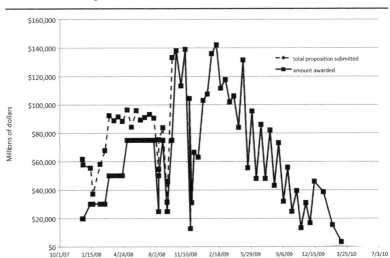

of June 2009. The offering amount gradually declined to $125 billion and then $100 billion in July and August 2009, and later fluctuated between $75 billion and $25 billion. The final auction was held on March 8, 2010 for $25 billion.

Although Figure 1 plots the offering amounts in each of the auctions and hence the potential (the supply of funds), it does not show the amount demanded by banks that submitted bids for TAF money or the amount that was actually loaned. Figure 2 supplements the information in Figure 1 by plotting both the total amount of proposition submitted by banks (the demand for loans) and the amount that was actually awarded.[8] As the figure illustrates, the demand for funds exceeded the supply from the first auction in December 2007 until the auction of September 22, 2008. For example, on December 12, 2007, the offering amount by the Federal Reserve was $20 billion, but the amount demanded by the 93 banks that submitted bids

---

[8] I use the notion of demand and supply here fairly loosely. Of course, given the auction structure, there was no excess demand at a given rate.

was $61.6 billion. In the auction of September 22, 2008, the facility was increased to $75 billion, but 85 banks submitted bids totaling $133.6 billion.

Following the Federal Reserve's increase of the facility size to $150 billion in October 2008, the amount of propositions submitted by banks dropped below the amount offered by the Federal Reserve until the end of the TAF. In the October 8, 2008 auction—the first auction with a facility size of $150 billion—71 banks submitted bids totaling $138.1 billion. The largest amount requested by banks was $142.5 billion, when 117 banks participated in the auction of February 9, 2009. The largest number of banks participating in a single auction was 124 (May 4, 2009), compared to only 16 banks on November 24, 2008.

4.3 TAF Lending to Foreign Banks

Table 5 lists the number of loans, average loan size, and total amount loaned in each month from the first auction in December 2007 through the final auction in March 2010. The table further breaks down monthly lending by whether the borrowing bank is a U.S. depository institution or a foreign bank.[9] Overall, foreign banks received 58 percent of the total amount lent over time, with a total amount of $2,214,688 million, compared to only $1,603,723 for U.S. banks. From December 2007 through most of 2008, foreign banks accounted for the vast majority of the lending, with amounts that were two to four times the total lending to U.S. banks. However, during the peak of the crisis and following the collapse of Lehman Brothers, and especially in October and November 2008, lending to U.S. banks exceeded borrowing by foreign banks. By April 2008 and until the end of the TAF, foreign banks again accounted for the majority of TAF lending.

Table 6 and Figure 3 present the 50 largest borrowers (measured by the total amount borrowed). For each of the largest borrowers, Table 6 lists the total loan amount, the average loan size, the number of loans obtained under the TAF, and the home country of the bank. Likewise, Figure 3 displays the largest 50 borrowers in a bar chart. As both Table 6 and Figure 3 show, UK-based Barclays is the largest borrower, with a total amount of $232,283 million in 49 loans, followed by Bank

---

[9] Foreign banks were eligible to participate in the TAF through their agencies or branches in the United States.

Table 5

Evolution of the TAF over Time: Domestic Banks vs. Foreign Banks

	Domestic Banks			Foreign Banks		
	Number of Loans	Average Loan Size (Millions)	Total Amount	Number of Loans	Average Loan Size (Millions)	Total Amount
December 2007	13	$374.9	$4,873	42	$836.4	$35,127
January 2008	46	$460.3	$21,172	35	$1,109.4	$38,828
February 2008	41	$423.6	$17,368	34	$1,253.9	$42,632
March 2008	45	$615.2	$27,683	41	$1,763.8	$72,318
April 2008	32	$487.5	$15,560	44	$1,918.2	$84,400
May 2008	76	$729.2	$55,418	56	$1,669.0	$94,581
June 2008	57	$848.0	$48,335	50	$2,033.3	$101,665
July 2008	105	$821.2	$86,230	79	$1,756.6	$138,770
August 2008	73	$912.7	$66,627	55	$1,515.9	$83,373
September 2008	40	$1,064.9	$42,595	46	$1,791.4	$82,405
October 2008	86	$1,730.4	$148,818	61	$1,681.1	$102,545
November 2008	113	$1,394.4	$157,561	60	$1,430.9	$85,856
December 2008	124	$608.2	$75,412	61	$1,602.9	$97,776
January 2009	185	$1,062.8	$196,617	89	$1,687.2	$150,160

February 2009	150	$1,025.6	$153,838	66	$1,519.7	$100,302
March 2009	149	$689.6	$102,743	71	$1,643.3	$116,672
April 2009	136	$608.4	$82,743	67	$1,602.8	$107,386
May 2009	159	$568.8	$90,446	61	$1,584.1	$96,633
June 2009	140	$258.5	$36,195	62	$1,723.5	$107,416
July 2009	210	$240.1	$50,417	87	$1,908.8	$166,062
August 2009	132	$192.2	$25,371	56	$1,624.5	$90,974
September 2009	109	$210.2	$22,912	49	$1,321.6	$64,759
October 2009	116	$192.5	$22,326	42	$1,001.7	$42,070
November 2009	104	$160.7	$16,713	31	$889.0	$27,558
December 2009	110	$155.8	$17,140	41	$1,112.8	$45,625
January 2010	98	$111.2	$10,893	23	$1,201.7	$27,638
February 2010	89	$64.8	$5,763	14	$690.2	$9,663
March 2010	49	$39.1	$1,915	4	$373.8	$1,495
December 2007–March 2010	**2,787**	**$575.4**	**$1,603,723**	**1,427**	**$1,552.0**	**$2,214,688**

Table 6
50 Largest Borrowers

Rank	Bank	Total Loan Amount (Millions)	Average Loan Size (Millions)	Number of Loans	Country
1	Barclays	$232,283	$4,740.5	49	UK
2	Bank of America	$212,617	$14,144.5	15	U.S.
3	Royal Bank of Scotland	$180,920	$4,523.0	40	UK
4	Wells Fargo	$153,953	$8,102.9	19	U.S.
5	Wachovia	$147,025	$6,392.4	23	U.S.
6	Société Générale	$124,377	$4,442.0	28	France
7	Dresdner Bank	$123,328	$3,333.2	37	Germany
8	RBS Citizens	$117,510	$4,039.7	29	U.S.
9	Citibank	$110,350	$4,244.2	26	U.S.
10	Bayerische Landesbank	$108,190	$2,924.1	37	Germany
11	Dexia	$105,167	$4,382.0	24	Belgium
12	Norinchukin Bank	$105,010	$3,281.6	32	Japan
13	JP Morgan Chase	$98,782	$4,939.1	20	U.S.
14	WestLB	$78,406	$2,178.0	36	UK
15	Deutsche Bank	$76,882	$3,844.1	20	Germany
16	Regions Bank	$72,444	$3,149.7	23	U.S.
17	Unicredit	$62,210	$2,592.1	24	Italy
18	Fortis Bank	$58,650	$1,725.0	34	Belgium
19	Sumitomo	$56,400	$1,151.0	49	Japan
20	UBS	$55,500	$3,468.8	16	Switzerland
21	Bank of Scotland	$53,500	$8,916.7	6	UK

(continued)

Table 6
(continued)

Rank	Bank	Total Loan Amount (Millions)	Average Loan Size (Millions)	Number of Loans	Country
22	HSH Nordbank	$52,550	$1,545.6	34	Germany
23	Mizuho	$51,284	$1,091.2	47	Japan
24	Commerzbank	$51,161	$2,046.5	25	Germany
25	Debfa Bank	$46,798	$2,600.0	18	Ireland
26	First Tennessee	$45,419	$1,297.7	35	U.S.
27	Fifth Third Bank	$44,478	$1,533.7	29	U.S.
28	State Bank	$42,000	$2,100.0	20	U.S.
29	Keybank	$40,214	$1,827.9	22	U.S.
30	DZ Bank	$39,477	$1,038.9	38	Germany
31	Citizens Bank	$39,380	$1,790.0	22	U.S.
32	Bank of Tokyo Mitsubishi	$35,900	$1,087.9	33	Japan
33	Royal Bank of Canada	$34,734	$1,085.4	32	Canada
34	Allied Irish	$34,700	$1,927.8	18	Ireland
35	Bayerische Hypo	$34,390	$802.1	43	Germany
36	Natixis	$32,817	$1,131.6	29	France
37	BNP Paribas	$31,275	$1,303.1	24	France
38	Toronto Dominion	$27,465	$1,445.5	19	Canada
39	Bank of Nova Scotia	$26,465	$661.6	40	Canada
40	Arab Banking Corporation	$26,350	$572.8	46	Bahrain
41	Standard Chartered	$25,100	$896.4	28	UK

(continued)

Table 6
(continued)

Rank	Bank	Total Loan Amount (Millions)	Average Loan Size (Millions)	Number of Loans	Country
42	Mitsubishi UFJ	$24,457	$444.7	55	Japan
43	Crédit Industriel et Commercial	$23,910	$703.2	34	France
44	Rabobank	$23,751	$2,375.0	10	Netherlands
45	BB&T	$22,700	$2,522.2	9	U.S.
46	Landesbank Baden	$22,580	$1,411.3	16	Germany
47	Ally Bank	$21,600	$1,963.6	11	U.S.
48	Marshall & Ilsley	$21,045	$841.8	25	U.S.
49	Countrywide	$20,750	$6,916.7	3	U.S.
50	Union Bank	$20,100	$1,182.4	17	U.S.

Figure 3
Largest TAF Borrowers

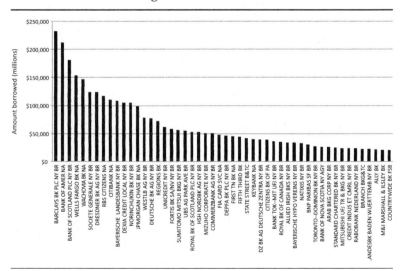

of America, with a total amount of $212,617 million in 15 loans. The next largest borrowers are Royal Bank of Scotland ($180,920 million), Wells Fargo ($153,953 million), and Wachovia ($147,025 million). Furthermore, out of the 10 largest borrowers, five are foreign banks, and out of the 50 largest borrowers, 33 are from foreign countries.

4.4 The Collateral Structure of Foreign Banks

As I argued previously, the loan term and interest rate were determined at the auction level regardless of the identity of the borrowing bank participating in the auction. In contrast, the size of the loan and the collateral pledged by the bank were the only margins that both the bank and the Federal Reserve could adjust at the loan level. Given the importance of collateral in general, and in particular given the unique setup of the TAF, I compared the collateral structure of domestic banks to the collateral used by foreign banks. Table 7 presents summary statistics on the use of collateral by domestic and foreign banks. For each asset category reported by the Federal Reserve, the table lists the mean share of the asset category in the collateral pool, the standard deviation of the share, and the number of loans pledging that asset as part of their collateral.

The summary statistics are reported separately for domestic and foreign banks, and a two-sample T-test for equal means is also presented. As Table 7 shows, foreign banks rarely used residential mortgages as collateral; only five loans made to foreign banks were secured by residential mortgages, compared to 460 loans to domestic banks. Conversely, ABSs were used in 983 loans to foreign banks, compared to 318 loans to domestic banks. Furthermore, ABSs account for a larger share of the overall collateral pool in foreign banks (9.323 versus 0.151, significant at the 1 percent level). As in the case of residential mortgages, foreign banks rarely used consumer loans (only 44) as collateral, while U.S.-based banks used consumer loans in 1,043 loans. Private MBSs and CMOs were more prevalent among foreign banks (although their share is slightly lower than in U.S. banks), and commercial real estate loans were used in only 222 foreign loans. Other significant differences between foreign and domestic banks are that foreign banks were less likely to use Agency MBSs and CMOs, U.S. Treasury/Agency securities, and U.S. municipal bonds and were much more likely to pledge international securities as collateral.

Table 7
Collateral Share: Domestic Banks vs. Foreign Banks

	Domestic Banks			Foreign Banks			Difference	Two-Sample T-test
	Mean	Standard Deviation	Number of Loans	Mean	Standard Deviation	Number of Loans		
Residential mortgages	0.280	0.01	460	0.733	0.01	5	-0.454	-3.37
Asset-backed securities	0.151	0.01	318	0.323	0.01	983	-0.172	-11.34
Commercial loans	0.470	0.01	1,656	0.427	0.02	635	0.043	2.83
Consumer loans	0.358	0.01	1,043	0.477	0.07	44	-0.119	-2.15
Private MBSs/CMOs	0.183	0.01	349	0.141	0.01	696	0.042	3.19
Commercial real estate	0.563	0.01	1,402	0.159	0.01	222	0.404	20.37
Corporate securities	0.192	0.01	428	0.265	0.01	1,079	-0.071	-4.74
International securities	0.133	0.02	194	0.208	0.01	944	-0.073	-3.83
Agency MBSs/CMOs	0.392	0.01	673	0.225	0.01	478	0.167	8.82
Municipals	0.233	0.01	611	0.055	0.01	488	0.177	12.26
U.S. Treasury/Agency	0.238	0.01	384	0.149	0.01	449	0.089	5.43

Table 8 supplements the results in Table 7 using regression analysis of the collateral composition of foreign banks. For each of the main asset categories, I use two dependent variables. The first dependent variable is a dummy variable for whether a security type is pledged as collateral for a particular loan. This variable captures the average tendency to use an asset as collateral. The second dependent variable is the actual share of the collateral in each asset group conditional on the asset being used as collateral. That is, while the first variable uses information on all loans, the second variable captures only the cross-sectional variation within an asset category conditional on its use. All regressions include year × month fixed-effects, as well as a control for the loan amount (in logs) and a dummy variable that takes the value of "1" for foreign banks, and "0" otherwise. Regressions for which the dependent variable is a dummy variable are estimated using probit where marginal effects are reported. Table 8 confirms the univariate findings. Foreign banks are more likely to use ABSs, international assets, and Treasuries, and are less likely to use commercial real estate.

5.   WHY FOREIGN BANKS?

Given that more than 58 percent of TAF lending went to foreign banks, it is important to understand why the Federal Reserve allocated its lending to foreign banks that are not under its direct supervision. In addition, the information contained in the collateral structure of these banks suggests that the collateral pledged by the foreign banks consisted of harder-to-value, riskier assets such as ABSs. In particular, the ABSs held by the foreign banks are—according to the data definitions provided by the Federal Reserve Board—collateralized debt obligations secured by ABSs, which were the securitized assets that declined the most during the crisis (Benmelech and Dlugosz 2009).

5.1   Exposure to Asset-Backed Securities

One potential explanation for both the elevated lending to foreign banks and their use of ABSs as collateral is that foreign banks were hit harder than U.S. banks and hence required more liquidity. Given that many foreign banks had exposure to assets that deteriorated in value (mostly ABSs and CDOs), these banks had weaker balance sheets.

Table 8
Collateral Composition of Foreign Banks

	Asset-Backed Securities		Commercial Real Estate		International Securities		Treasury Securities	
	Extensive	Intensive	Extensive	Intensive	Extensive	Intensive	Extensive	Intensive
Log (loan amount)	0.090***	0.025***	0.034***	−0.072***	0.018***	−0.008*	0.006*	−0.064***
	(0.004)	(0.005)	(0.004)	(0.003)	(0.004)	(0.005)	(0.004)	(0.005)
Foreign dummy	0.393***	0.143***	−0.403***	−0.231***	0.611***	0.136***	0.178***	0.082***
	(0.018)	(0.015)	(0.015)	(0.018)	(0.017)	(0.021)	(0.016)	(0.015)
Fixed-effects								
Year × Month	Yes	Yes	Yes	Yes	Yes	Yes	Yes	Yes
Pseudo / Adjusted R^2	0.39	0.13	0.11	0.41	0.39	0.09	0.05	0.26
Observations	4,214	1,301	4,214	1,624	4,214	1,138	4,214	833

Note: * = 10% significance level; ** = 5% significance level; *** = 1% significance level. Standard errors in parentheses.

However, foreign banks were not the only banks exposed to ABS CDOs. Table 9 provides information on aggregate crisis-related write-downs as well as write-downs for some of the largest financial institutions in the world.[10] As the table demonstrates, as of October 2008, Citigroup had written down $34.1 billion as a result of exposure to ABS CDOs, followed by Merrill Lynch ($26.1 billion) and Bank of America ($9.1 billion). As of February 2009, the total value of write-downs by financial institutions around the world was $520.1 billion, out of which $218.2 billion were due to exposure to ABS CDOs, representing 42 percent of total write-downs by the financial sector. Write-downs driven by ABS CDOs were more than four times the size of corporate credit-related write-downs. North American banks accounted for the largest share of ABS CDO write-downs, followed by European banks. The European bank with the largest exposure to ABSs was UBS ($21,870 million), followed by Fortis Bank ($4,359 million), Royal Bank of Scotland ($3,609 million), and Deutsche Bank ($2,092 million).

If banks that had worse balance sheets because of exposure to structured finance products were more likely to participate in the TAF, we should expect the institutions with the most exposure to ABS CDOs to borrow more under the TAF and pledge those securities as collateral. However, mere exposure to structured finance assets does not seem to explain either the amount of borrowing or the collateral used by the banks.

Table 10 lists the 50 banks that pledged the largest amounts of ABSs per loan. As the table clearly shows, and consistent with Tables 7 and 8, most of the banks and financial institutions that pledged ABSs as collateral were foreign—mostly European—banks. For example, the bank that pledged the largest amount of ABSs for a given loan was Société Générale (France), followed by Norinchukin Bank (Japan), Dexia (Belgium), Barclays (UK), and UBS (Switzerland). Among the 10 banks that pledged the largest amounts of ABSs as collateral, only two were American banks (State Street and U.S. Central Federal Credit Union).

In contrast, the American banks that had the largest exposure and write-downs because of ABS CDOs—Citigroup and Bank of America—had only modest borrowing secured by ABSs. For

---

[10] The data are from Creditflux, a leading information source globally for credit trading and investing, credit derivatives, structured credit, distressed credit, and credit research. This table is based on the results presented in Benmelech and Dlugosz (2009).

Table 9
ABS CDOs and Write-Downs

Panel A: Crisis-Related Write-Downs for Selected Banks (Millions)

	ABS CDOs	Corporate Credit	RMBS	Other	Total
North American Banks					
Bank of America	$9,089	$932	–	$2,834	$12,855
Bear Stearns	$2,300	–	–	–	$2,300
Citigroup	$34,106	$4,053	$1,319	$15,904	$55,382
Goldman Sachs	–	$4,100	$1,700	$1,400	$7,200
JP Morgan Chase	$1,300	$5,467	$5,305	–	$12,072
Lehman Brothers	$200	$1,300	$4,100	$3,400	$9,000
Merrill Lynch	$26,100	$2,845	$12,998	$13,125	$55,068
Morgan Stanley	$7,800	$3,810	$3,781	$1,992	$17,383
European Banks					
Credit Suisse	$3,427	$3,057	$530	$2,523	$9,357
Deutsche Bank	$2,092	$5,820	$3,386	$3,677	$14,974
Fortis Bank	$4,359	$3,660	$144	–	$8,163
ING	$565	–	$8,028	$25	$8,617
Royal Bank of Scotland	$3,609	$1,849	$2,566	$4,122	$12,146
UBS	$21,870	$348	$1,716	$13,871	$37,805
Asian and Emerging Market Banks					
Aozora Bank	$510	–	–	–	$510
Mitsubishi UFJ	$360	$2,348	$921	$11	$3,640
Mizuho	$3,898	$629	$2,539	$584	$7,650
National Australia Bank	$670	–	–	–	$670
Sumitomo Mitsui	$562	–	–	–	$562

(continued)

Table 9
(continued)

Panel B: Aggregate Crisis-Related Write-Downs (Millions)

	ABS CDOs	Corporate Credit	RMBS	Other	Total
North American	$84,319	$23,702	$42,272	$59,011	$209,305
European	$63,464	$18,579	$26,423	$62,634	$171,100
Asian and Emerging Markets	$9,358	$4,724	$5,728	$3,743	$23,553
TOTAL	$218,216	$53,324	$84,810	$163,735	$520,084

example, as Table 9 demonstrates, Citibank had the largest write-downs due to ABS CDOs borrowed against $760.8 million of ABSs, compared to Société Générale with $16,352.0 million and UBS with $9,419.0 million. Thus, despite their exposure to ABSs and structured finance assets, American banks were less likely to obtain term funding through the TAF or to pledge ABSs as collateral.

5.2 The European Banks' Dollar Crisis

Another explanation for the large number of loans made to foreign banks is that these banks suffered from a currency mismatch in their balance sheets. Many foreign banks were active players in the creation and issuance of structured finance products. As money markets came to a halt, these banks required financing to meet the needs of rolling over their short-term liabilities. Foreign banks were also subject to a currency mismatch in managing their assets and liabilities. Although the main source of funding for some of these banks was demand deposits and other forms of credit in their home countries that were denominated in their home currencies (mostly the British pound and the euro), many European banks issued liabilities in U.S. money markets that were denominated in the U.S. dollar. Thus, not only were foreign banks subject to a roll-over risk, they also suffered from a currency mismatch and had to rely on special facilities such as the currency swap lines between central banks, including the European Central Bank, Bank of England, Swiss National Bank, and Federal Reserve, as well as special lending programs such as the TAF.

Table 10
Banks Pledging Most Asset-Backed Securities

Rank	Bank	ABS Amount (Millions)	Country
1	Société Générale	$16,532.0	France
2	Norinchukin Bank	$14,607.9	Japan
3	Dexia	$11,429.7	Belgium
4	Barclays	$9,805.1	UK
5	UBS	$9,419.0	Switzerland
6	State Street	$9,125.6	U.S.
7	Royal Bank of Scotland	$8,227.8	UK
8	Bank of Scotland	$6,518.5	UK
9	U.S. Central Federal Credit Union	$5,293.2	U.S.
10	Bank of Tokyo Mitsubishi	$4,650.5	Japan
11	Depfa Bank	$3,405.0	Ireland
12	Abbey National Treasury	$3,143.3	UK
13	Bayerische Landesbank	$2,605.4	Germany
14	Deutsche Bank	$2,590.0	Germany
15	Landesbank Baden	$2,505.4	Germany
16	WestLB	$2,096.3	UK
17	HSH Nordbank	$2,028.8	Germany
18	Calyon	$1,904.7	France
19	Shinkin Central Bank	$1,824.0	Japan
20	DZ Bank	$1,496.5	Germany
21	Skandinaviska Enskilda	$1,444.3	Sweden
22	Dresdner Bank	$1,436.3	Germany
23	PNC Bank	$1,390.9	U.S.
24	Natixis	$1,308.3	France
25	Sumitomo	$959.0	Japan
26	Washington Mutual	$920.2	U.S.
27	Erste Bank	$884.1	Austria
28	Standard Chartered	$869.3	UK

(continued)

Table 10
(continued)

29	Fortis Bank	$838.4	Belgium
30	Royal Bank of Canada	$802.0	Canada
31	Allied Irish	$770.5	Ireland
32	HSBC	$761.0	UK
33	Citibank	$760.8	U.S.
34	Fifth Third Bank	$736.8	U.S.
35	Bank of Montreal	$667.7	Canada
36	Commerzbank	$565.0	Germany
37	Mizuho	$510.3	Japan
38	Metlife	$504.3	U.S.
39	Sallie Mae	$503.0	U.S.
40	Zions First National Bank	$426.3	U.S.
41	RBC Bank	$417.5	U.S.
42	Advanta	$236.6	U.S.
43	Crédit Industriel et Commercial	$226.3	France
44	Ally Bank	$194.8	U.S.
45	Mitsubishi UFJ	$192.1	Japan
46	First Hawaiian Bank	$155.0	U.S.
47	Bank Hapoalim	$149.3	Israel
48	California National Bank	$113.0	U.S.
49	Norddeutsche Landesbank	$92.2	Germany
50	M&T Bank	$89.7	U.S.

Foreign banks played an important role in American financial markets during the years leading up to the financial crisis. According to Shin (2011, 3): "The U.S. dollar–denominated assets of banks outside the United States are comparable in size to the total assets of the U.S. commercial banking sector, peaking at over $10 trillion prior to the crisis. The [Bank for International Settlements] banking statistics reveal that a substantial portion of external U.S. dollar claims are the claims of European banks against U.S. counterparties." Likewise, studies from the Bank for International Settlements by Baba, McCauley, and Ramaswamy (2009) and McGuire and von Peter (2009) show that U.S. dollar wholesale deposits and money market funds were an important source of funding for European global banks in the years leading to the crisis.

Moreover, Shin (2011) provides evidence that European global banks raised their assets in the United States in the years leading to the crisis, increasing their claims against U.S. borrowers by almost 40 percent from 2005 to 2007. Although European banks had access to U.S. credit markets, they still had their core funding in their home countries in European currencies. This currency mismatch between their assets—many in the form of private-label ABSs and CDOs—and their liabilities is what made them vulnerable to the halt in U.S. short-term lending markets.

According to this view, European banks were more likely to bid for TAF money because they were affected more severely by the financial crisis, given their exposure to a currency mismatch between assets and liabilities. Shin draws similar conclusions from the fact that a large fraction of TAF lending went to European banks. He writes:

> Two features stand out from the charts in Figure 11. The first is that the non-U.S. banks' total borrowing is large relative to U.S. banks' borrowing. The relative magnitudes are roughly comparable at the peak. The second feature that stands out is the preponderance of European banks in the list of non-U.S. recipients of TAF funding. The UK banks are especially prominent, led by Barclays, RBS, and Bank of Scotland. The list also reveals some unlikely names, such as Norinchukin (the Agricultural Savings Bank of Japan) and the German landesbanks, who are likely to have ventured into U.S. dollar lending in their search for higher yielding assets to deploy their large domestic deposit bases. (Shin 2011, 17–18)

Thus, the elevated lending to foreign banks and in particular to European banks likely reflects their prominent role in the U.S. financial system, their involvement in the structured finance markets (especially the private-name ABSs and CDOs), and the currency mismatch in their balance sheets.

6. CONCLUSION

This paper provides detailed analysis of the TAF plan using micro-level data on the individual loans, the assets posted as collateral, and the identity of the borrowing banks. I found that foreign banks accounted for about 60 percent of TAF lending and that the largest borrowers in the program were mostly European banks. Moreover, most of the banks that pledged ABSs as collateral were European banks.

I argue that the main reason for the large number of loans made to foreign banks was the currency mismatch in European banks' balance sheets. Many European banks were active players in the creation and issuance of structured finance products, and as money markets came to a halt, these banks required financing to roll over their short-term liabilities. These European banks also faced a currency mismatch in managing their assets and liabilities. Although the main source of funding for some of these banks was based on demand deposits and other forms of credit in their home countries that were denominated in their home currencies, they issued liabilities in U.S. money markets that were denominated in the U.S. dollar. Thus, foreign banks not only were subject to a roll-over risk but also suffered from a currency mismatch and had to rely on special facilities such as the TAF.

The data illustrate the scale of the operation of foreign—in particular European—banks in U.S. financial markets. What precise role do European banks play in the American economy? What led to their involvement in the U.S. financial system? These questions are left for future research.

REFERENCES

Baba, Naohiko, Robert N. McCauley, and Srichander Ramaswamy. 2009. "U.S. Dollar Money Market Funds and Non-U.S. Banks." *BIS Quarterly Review* March: 65–81.

Benmelech, Efraim, and Jennifer Dlugosz. 2009. "The Credit Rating Crisis." *NBER Macroeconomics Annual* 26: 161–207.

Bernanke, Ben. 2009. "The Federal Reserve's Balance Sheet: An Update." Speech at the Federal Reserve Board Conference on Key Developments in Monetary Policy. Washington, D.C. October 8.

McAndrews, James, Asani Sarkar, and Zhenyu Wang. 2008. "The Effect of the Term Auction Facility on the London Inter-Bank Offered Rate." Staff Report no. 335. Federal Reserve Bank of New York.

McGuire, Patrick, and Goetz von Peter. 2009. "The U.S. Dollar Shortage in Global Banking." *BIS Quarterly Review* March: 47–63.

Shin, Hyun Song. 2011. "Global Banking Glut and Loan Risk Premium." 2011. Mundell-Fleming Lecture Conference Draft. Paper presented at the 12th Jacques Polak Annual Research Conference. Washington, D.C.: International Monetary Fund.

Taylor, John B., and John C. Williams. 2009. "A Black Swan in the Money Market." *American Economic Journal: Macroeconomic* 1 (1): 58–83.

Comment

Simon Gilchrist

Efraim Benmelech's paper presents a welcome overview and analysis of the Federal Reserve's Term Auction Facility (TAF) based on the micro lending data recently made available by the Federal Reserve. The paper documents both the size of loans received and the forms of collateral that were pledged. It also highlights the fact that foreign banks were large recipients of TAF funds throughout the financial crisis.

The TAF was one of many policy initiatives put in place by the Federal Reserve to combat financial market turmoil since the onset of the financial crisis. Some of these programs represent conventional monetary policy measures, aimed directly at increasing overall market liquidity and reducing interest rates via the purchase of safe-asset securities such as Treasury bonds, mortgage-backed securities, and agency debt. In the early stages of the crisis, interest rates were reduced via standard open market operations combined with reductions in the primary credit rate obtained through borrowing at the discount window. In later stages of the crisis, with the effective Fed funds rate at the zero lower bound, the Federal Reserve conducted large-scale asset purchases (quantitative easing) to reduce long-term interest rates relative to short-term interest rates. It also provided extensive guidance on the future path of short-term interest rates.

In contrast, other programs pursued by the Federal Reserve are better viewed as unconventional, in the sense that they are more closely linked to credit than to monetary policy. These include the extension of liquidity to primary dealers (through the Term Securities Lending Facility and the Primary Dealer Credit Facility), the provision of liquidity to the private sector (through direct lending

Simon Gilchrist is professor of economics at Boston University and a research associate of the National Bureau of Economic Research.

programs such as the asset-backed commercial paper/money market funds liquidity facility, the commercial paper funding facility, the money market investor funding facility, the term asset-backed securities loan facility), and the direct bailout of financial institutions such as Bear-Stearns and AIG.

The TAF is a straightforward extension of discount window lending and therefore should be understood as part of the traditional tool kit of the monetary authority. It differed from discount window lending in the anonymous nature of the auction, which was designed to reduce any perceived stigma associated with such borrowing. It also potentially differed from discount window lending in that the primary credit rate was the minimum bid rate but not necessarily the effective borrowing rate. Thus, the TAF gave the Federal Reserve the potential to "price-discriminate" between the two forms of borrowing. Indeed, one of the interesting facts documented in the paper is that the auctions were over-subscribed prior to September 2008 but under-subscribed thereafter. In effect, prior to September 2008, the Fed controlled the aggregate quantity of borrowing and let the price adjust to market conditions. Because the borrowing rate was higher than the primary (minimum bid) rate during this period, banks effectively viewed discount window borrowing as carrying a stigma. Indeed, the difference between the bid rate and the primary rate provides a lower bound on the premium placed on anonymity during this time period. Post–September 2008, the Fed set the price at the primary rate and effectively let banks borrow freely at that rate via the TAF program.

As emphasized by Benmelech's paper, another important aspect of the TAF program is the amount and type of collateral that was posted. The paper documents that the amount and type is bank-specific, with foreign banks more likely to post what appears to be riskier collateral. Because one cannot observe the haircuts applied to different asset classes when determining eligible collateral, it is not really feasible to infer the risk structure of such loans based on posted collateral. The paper also suggests that the collateral requirements may be an important tool that the Fed could use in its conduct of monetary policy. Two reasons for caution emerge: First, the available collateral, and therefore haircuts, are determined in the same manner as borrowing at the discount window; both are therefore set by the individual Reserve Banks within whose district a bank would borrow. It is unlikely that the Federal Reserve actively manipulated these requirements from one auction to the next or sought to apply haircuts differentially across foreign versus domestic banks. Second, in nearly all cases, the amount of collateral posted greatly exceeds the amount borrowed. Thus, it is difficult to view the collateral postings as representative of the marginal value of an additional unit of collateral that may vary systematically across banks. Indeed, differences in the type of collateral posted across foreign versus domestic banks likely reflect the type of assets held by the banks. Thus, for example, the relatively low usage of residential mortgages as collateral by foreign banks simply reflects the fact that these banks are not actively engaged in the residential mortgage business in the United States.

The main thrust of the paper is to highlight the importance of borrowing by foreign banks under the TAF program. Any foreign bank that is regulated as a foreign branch or U.S. subsidiary is eligible to borrow at the discount window and therefore through the TAF program. As emphasized in the paper, the fact that foreign banks found it desirable to do so must, to a great extent, reflect the overall need for dollar funding in international money markets. Such funding became increasingly scarce as the interbank markets ceased to function during the depth of the financial crisis. The extent of borrowing by foreign banks may also indicate that, relative to the alternative, the TAF program offered a good deal in terms of lending against collateral that would otherwise not be accepted in the marketplace or, for that matter, as collateral by the European Central Bank during this time period.

From this perspective, it is useful to ask what are the consequences and policy tradeoffs associated with the TAF program. The Federal Reserve clearly decided that providing dollar funding was an important tool in its tool kit during the crisis. Indeed, the provision of dollar funding through swap lines to the European Central Bank and other central banks accounted for the largest share of the Federal Reserve's balance sheet at the height of the crisis. Are swap lines the desirable alternative? To the extent that haircuts were not sufficient, the heavy use of the TAF program by foreign banks likely exposed the Federal Reserve to additional risk from European banks. Swap lines reduce the Federal Reserve's exposure to foreign-bank risks but increase its exposure to sovereign risk. The costs and benefits of such a tradeoff are highly relevant to policymakers in today's environment where markets perceive little difference between bank and sovereign risk.

Comment

Ross Levine

During an extraordinary period in the economic and financial history of the United States, a period when the familiar tools of monetary policy did not function, the Federal Reserve developed and implemented new procedures for addressing the liquidity problems plaguing banks. In particular, by the end of 2007, banks had become worried about the creditworthiness of other banks, uncertain about their own ability to borrow in the future, and consequently exceedingly reluctant to lend to other banks. This breakdown in interbank lending disrupted the normal functioning of open market operations, which relies on banks that sell securities to the Federal Reserve to then lend excess funds to other banks instead of simply accumulating excess reserves at the Fed.

With one monetary policy tool malfunctioning, the Fed attempted to employ another traditional tool: lending funds directly to banks through the discount window. But the stigma associated with borrowing from the Fed—the view that only weak banks use the discount window—meant that banks were disinclined to use the discount window, hindering the efficacy of this monetary policy tool as well. Thus, the Fed faced a challenge: it viewed the burgeoning financial crisis as emanating from the liquidity problems plaguing banks, but its traditional tools for addressing the problem did not work. So it created new tools.

One of the first new tools that the Fed developed to ease liquidity problems was the Term Auction Facility (TAF), which started in December of 2007 and ceased operations in March of 2010. At its peak, the TAF was almost a $500 billion item on the Fed's balance sheet. Under the TAF, the Fed would choose a quantity of money to auction to banks. All banks that were eligible to borrow under the Fed's traditional

Ross Levine is the Willis H. Booth Chair in Banking and Finance in the Haas School of Business at the University of California, Berkeley, a senior fellow at the Milken Institute, and a research associate of the National Bureau of Economic Research.

primary credit program were also eligible to participate in the new TAF. Banks would submit quantity/interest rate offers. Subject to its traditional collateral requirements, TAF funds would then be allocated in a mechanical manner beginning with those banks offering the highest rates. Initially, the Fed kept the identity of borrowing banks secret so as to avoid any stigma associated with borrowing from the Fed.

In a valuable contribution to understanding Federal Reserve policies during the recent financial crisis, Efraim Benmelech provides detailed information on how individual banks used the TAF program. In particular, Benmelech documents that

- Almost 60 percent of TAF funds flowed to foreign banks.
- The foreign banks pledged a larger proportion of asset-backed securities as collateral than did domestic banks.

Benmelech also provides suggestive evidence that foreign banks were more aggressive in bidding for TAF funds than domestic banks were; the foreign banks needed to meet their dollar-denominated liabilities and were more limited in their options for obtaining dollar funds. Benmelech does a superb job of documenting which banks used the TAF and the conditions of that use. His work provides vital inputs into the long process of evaluating the Fed's response to the crisis.

Many questions remain. In terms of Benmelech's specific analyses, while it is interesting to know that more than half of TAF funds flowed to foreign banks, what are the policy implications of this observation? And while it is noteworthy that foreign banks pledged different types of collateral than those pledged by U.S. banks, what does this mean for bank behavior? At a broader level, did the TAF ease liquidity constraints and, if so, was it a cost-effective tool for achieving this goal?

Moreover, since the TAF was only one of the many new tools developed by the Fed in response to the novel circumstances of the period from 2007 to 2009, it should be evaluated within the broader context of the Fed's overall response to the crisis. Indeed, the massive purchase of agency and agency-guaranteed mortgage-backed securities was several times larger than the TAF; other programs—such as the term asset-backed securities loan facility and the central bank liquidity swaps—were more narrowly targeted at specific segments of the financial system. Thus, looking at the TAF in particular might yield misleading information about the Fed's overall strategy for addressing the problems facing banks during the period from 2007 through 2010.

Executive Compensation and Corporate Governance in the United States: Perceptions, Facts, and Challenges

Steven N. Kaplan

ABSTRACT

In this paper, I consider the evidence for three common perceptions of U.S. chief executive officer (CEO) pay and corporate governance: (1) CEOs are overpaid and their pay keeps increasing; (2) CEOs are not paid for their performance; and (3) boards do not penalize CEOs for poor performance. While average CEO pay increased substantially through the 1990s, it has declined since then. CEO pay levels relative to other highly paid groups today are comparable to their average levels in the early 1990s. The ratio of large-company CEO pay to firm market value also is similar to its level in the late 1970s and lower than its pre-1960s levels. The relative pay of large-company CEOs in the late 2000s is comparable to or modestly higher than in the late 1930s. This all suggests that similar forces, likely technology and scale, have played a meaningful role in driving CEO pay and the pay of others with top incomes. With regard to performance, CEOs are paid for performance and penalized for poor performance. Finally, boards do monitor CEOs. The rate of CEO turnover has increased in the 2000s, compared to the 1980s and 1990s, and is significantly tied to poor stock performance. While corporate governance failures and pay outliers—as well as the very high average pay levels relative to the typical household—undoubtedly have contributed to the common perceptions, a meaningful part of CEO pay appears to be market-determined and boards do appear to monitor their CEOs. Consistent with that finding, top executive pay policies at over 98 percent of S&P 500 and Russell 3000 companies received majority shareholder support in the Dodd-Frank mandated "say-on-pay" votes in 2011.

Steven N. Kaplan is the Neubauer Family Distinguished Service Professor of Entrepreneurship and Finance in the Booth School of Business at the University of Chicago. He is also a research associate of the National Bureau of Economic Research, and he serves on public company and mutual fund boards.

The author thanks Douglas Baird, Effi Benmelech, Carola Frydman, Austan Goolsbee, Jeff Miron, Raghu Rajan, Amir Sufi, Luke Taylor, and Rob Vishny for helpful comments.

Executive Compensation and Corporate Governance in the United States: Perceptions, Facts, and Challenges

1. INTRODUCTION

Chief executive officers (CEOs) are routinely perceived to be over-paid, and corporate boards of directors are perceived to provide poor or limited oversight of CEOs. These perceptions have three typical components:

- CEOs are overpaid and their pay keeps increasing.
- CEOs are not paid for their performance.
- Boards are not doing their jobs as monitors.

For example, Bebchuk and Fried (2006) claim that "flawed compensation arrangements have not been limited to a small number of 'bad apples'; they have been widespread, persistent, and systemic."

In the last decade, the United States has implemented two major pieces of legislation designed to improve corporate governance. The scandals of Enron, WorldCom, and others early in this century led to the Sarbanes-Oxley legislation in 2002. The subsequent financial crisis led to the Dodd-Frank legislation in 2010, which includes a requirement that all public companies obtain an annual advisory shareholder vote on top executive pay ("say-on-pay"). Despite the legislation and attention, the perceptions and criticism of CEO pay continue. Recently, the *New York Times* wrote, "[T]he top brass generally do much, much better than the rest of us, whether times are good or bad."[1] And *Forbes* wrote, "Our report on executive compensation will only fuel the outrage over corporate greed."[2]

In this paper, I consider the accuracy of these perceptions today. What are the facts about CEO pay? Is it true that the typical CEO is

---

[1] Natalie Singer. "A Rich Game of Thrones: C.E.O. Pay Gains May Have Slowed, but the Numbers Are Still Numbing." *New York Times*. April 8, 2012.

[2] Scott DeCarlo. "Gravity-Defying CEO Pay." *Forbes*. April 23, 2012.

not paid for performance? How much and how well do public company boards monitor their CEOs, particularly for poor performance? The recurring question I address is what are the drivers of CEO pay? Is pay driven by the power that CEOs wield over their boards, leading CEOs to be overpaid? Is pay driven by a competitive market for talent, such that CEOs are paid appropriately? Or is pay driven by a combination of those and other forces?

What has happened to CEO pay over time? CEO pay can be measured in two ways. The first, "estimated" or "grant-date" pay, includes the CEO's salary, bonus, restricted stock, and the estimated value of stock options when they are granted. This is the compensation package the board has awarded the CEO that year. The second, "realized" pay, values stock options at their realized values only if and when they are exercised and realized.

In looking at CEO pay levels, I focus on estimated pay because that is the pay under the board's control. Average estimated CEO pay (adjusted for inflation) is at roughly the same level in 2010 as it was in 1998 and lower than it was in 2000. In other words, average CEO pay has not continued to increase. It has declined since the large run-up of the 1990s.

While public company CEO pay has declined, it is still very high relative to typical household income. But that is also true of the pay of top performers in other professions such as lawyers, investors, and private company executives. I extend the analysis in Kaplan and Rauh (2010) to measure average CEO pay relative to the pay of others with top incomes. The ratio of average CEO pay to the average pay of those with top incomes (the top 0.1 percent of taxpayers, annually) is comparable to or lower than the ratios in the early 1990s. The ratio in the late 2000s is comparable to (albeit slightly higher than) the level in the late 1930s.[3] And the results in Bakija, Cole, and Heim (2012) suggest that the pay of public company executives has increased by less than the pay of private company executives.

I also extend the analysis in Kaplan and Rauh (2010) to show the increase in compensation for several particular highly paid groups. Top lawyers have seen their pay increase by roughly the same percentage as the CEOs of firms in Standard and Poor's 500–stock index.

---

[3] See also Murphy (2012) and Frydman and Jenter (2010) for excellent surveys on CEO pay. They show similar time series evidence on CEO compensation.

Hedge fund, private equity, and venture capital investors have seen their fees increase markedly. The top 25 hedge fund managers as a group regularly earn more than all 500 CEOs in the S&P 500.

In other words, while public company CEOs are highly paid, other groups with similar backgrounds and talents have done at least equally well over the last 15–20 years. If one uses evidence of higher CEO pay as evidence of managerial power or capture, one must also explain why the other professional groups have had a similar or even higher growth in pay. A more natural interpretation is that the market for talent has driven a meaningful portion of the increase in pay at the top. Consistent with this market-determined conclusion, top executive pay policies at more than 98 percent of firms in the S&P 500 and Russell Investments' 3000-stock index received majority shareholder support in the Dodd-Frank mandated say-on-pay votes in 2011. The 2012 votes have followed a similar pattern.

Second, are CEOs paid for good stock performance? In looking at CEO pay-for-performance, I look at the relation of realized pay to firm performance. The question is whether CEOs who perform better earn more in realized pay. Kaplan and Rauh (2010) look at actual CEO pay in a given year. Firms with CEOs in the top quintile (top 20 percent) of realized pay generate stock returns 60 percent greater than those of other firms in their industries over the previous three years. Firms with CEOs in the bottom quintile of realized pay underperform their industries by almost 20 percent in the previous three years. The results are qualitatively similar with performance over the previous five years or previous year. The important question that is harder to answer is whether the extent of that pay-for-performance is efficient and appropriate given market conditions.

Third, are boards doing their jobs? Kaplan and Minton (2012) study CEO turnover among firms appearing in *Fortune* magazine's annual list of the 500 largest grossing U.S. companies from 1992 to 2007. Turnover levels for these firms since 1998 have been higher than in work that has studied earlier periods. In any given year, one out of six *Fortune* 500 CEOs loses his or her job. This compares to one out of 10 in the 1970s. CEOs can expect to be CEOs for less time than in the past. If these declines in expected CEO tenures since 1998 are factored in, the effective decline in CEO pay since then is larger than reported above.

And the CEO turnover is related to poor firm stock performance— both poor performance relative to the industry and poor industry performance. Jenter and Llewellen (2010) present additional evidence consistent with this conclusion. They find "that boards aggressively fire CEOs for poor performance, and that the turnover-performance sensitivity increases substantially with board quality" (boards with more independent directors and more director stock ownership).

Murphy (2012) ends his impressive and detailed survey of executive compensation with the conclusion that "[i]t's complicated." He concludes that executive compensation is affected by the interaction of a competitive market for talent, managerial power, and political factors. His conclusion is hard to disagree with, and the data I present here are consistent with it.

Of course, corporate governance failures do occur, and pay outliers where managerial power is exercised can surely be found. And, again, the pay levels discussed here are very high relative to the typical household. These factors undoubtedly feed the common perceptions. In addition, political and tax factors likely have contributed to the run-up of pay in the 1990s and the decline since then.

However, the average, large sample, and long-term evidence are less consistent with the common perceptions and more supportive of market forces as important determinants of CEO pay levels. CEO pay in particular is likely to have been affected by forces similar to those that have led to the increase in incomes at the very top. At the same time, boards *have* been performing their monitoring function—and arguably have been doing so better today than in previous decades. The positive results of the 2011 (and 2012) say-on-pay votes suggest a meaningful role for a competitive market for talent.

This evidence also explains why compensation and the role of boards are likely to remain challenging, if not controversial. While boards have to pay well enough to attract and retain executive talent, they must be sensitive to the accurate perception that CEO pay is high relative to the median household and to the negative publicity from pay and governance outliers.

The rest of this paper details these results and conclusions.

2.   HOW IS CEO PAY MEASURED?

CEO and top executive pay can be measured two ways. The first measure is the estimated or grant-date value of CEO pay. This includes the CEO's salary and bonus, the value of restricted stock issued, and the estimated value of the options issued to the CEO that year (usually calculated using the Black-Scholes option pricing model, a generally accepted formula for valuing options). This is the compensation package the board has awarded the CEO that year and, therefore, the appropriate measure to estimate pay levels and assess board governance.

Estimated pay is not a measure of what the CEO actually gets to take home. The CEO takes his or her salary and bonus, but does not get to cash in the options or the restricted stock. Estimated pay, therefore, is not the appropriate measure for considering whether CEOs are paid for performance.[4]

The second measure is realized or actual CEO pay. This includes the CEO's salary and bonus, the value of restricted stock, and the value of the options the CEO exercised that year. Because it uses actual option gains (not the theoretical values), this second measure is a better measure of the amount of money the CEO actually takes home in a given year. This measure, therefore, is more appropriate for considering whether CEOs are paid for performance.[5]

Note that realized pay is not a perfect measure, because it includes restricted stock granted in a year as realized pay. In reality, the restricted stock vests over time, so executives cannot sell their restricted stock for several years. As a result, even realized pay may understate the extent to which CEOs are paid for performance.

Another point worth remembering is that the realized pay measure does not necessarily include the options granted in just one year. That is, in any given year, a CEO may choose to exercise options granted over many years or may choose not to exercise any options. As a result, realized pay will tend to be more variable than estimated pay.

3. WHAT ARE THE FACTS ABOUT CEO PAY?

In this section, I report time series information on the pay of U.S. CEOs. I begin with the CEOs of S&P 500 companies from 1993 to 2010 using data from Standard and Poor's ExecuComp database. These are the largest publicly traded U.S. companies, with the median

---

[4] It is interesting and somewhat puzzling that Institutional Shareholder Services (ISS), the prominent proxy advisory firm, uses estimated pay to assess pay-for-performance. See Hewitt and Bowie (2011) for ISS's perspective on pay-for-performance.

[5] Because it measures realized gains, it also includes any benefits from backdating that lowered the exercise price of the options.

S&P 500 company employing more than 20,000 people. I then report pay for the CEOs of the other companies covered by ExecuComp—companies that at one time have been in Standard and Poor's 1500-stock index but are not in the S&P 500. For both sets of companies, I consider estimated and realized pay.

3.1 S&P 500 CEOs

Figures 1 through 4 report information on the pay of S&P 500 CEOs from 1993 to 2010. The figures show that CEO pay increased significantly from 1993 to 2000. Since 2000, however, average CEO pay has declined. In real terms, pay in 2010 was roughly equal to its level in 1998.

Figure 1 reports the average and median total estimated pay of S&P 500 CEOs from 1993 to 2010 (in millions of 2010 dollars). This is the pay the board expects to give the CEO. Average CEO pay increased markedly from 1993 to 2000. Since peaking in 2000, it has declined by more than 46 percent. Median CEO pay also increased markedly from 1993 to 2000. Median pay peaked in 2001 and has declined slightly since then. The convergence of the means

Figure 1
Average and Median Total Pay of S&P 500 CEOs, 1993–2010 (estimated; in millions of 2010 dollars)

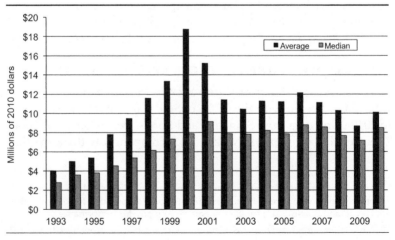

Source: ExecuComp.

Figure 2
Average and Median Total Pay of S&P 500 CEOs Relative
to Median Household Income, 1993–2010 (estimated)

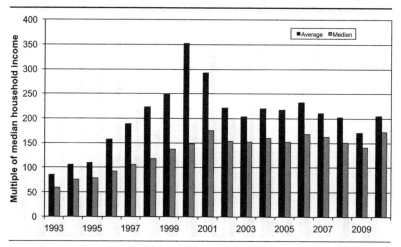

Sources: ExecuComp, Census Accounts.

and medians suggests that boards have become substantially less likely to award large and unusual pay packages to CEOs since 2000. Nevertheless, the graphs indicate that boards expected to pay CEOs well. In 2010, among S&P 500 CEOs, the median estimated pay was just over $8.5 million; the average pay was just over $10 million.

Figure 2 reports S&P 500 CEO estimated pay relative to median household income. Again, average and median CEO pay peaked in 2000–2001. Average CEO pay peaked in 2000 at more than 350 times the median household income in the United States. It has since declined to roughly 200 times. Median CEO pay peaked in 2001 at somewhat more than 175 times median household income, and that number has remained more or less constant. While these multiples are not as high as some that are quoted by shareholder activists, they remain very high.[6]

[6] For example, as of April 2012, the AFL-CIO website reports that CEO pay in 2010 was 343 times that of the median worker.

Figure 3
Average and Median Total Pay of S&P 500 CEOs,
1993–2010 (realized)

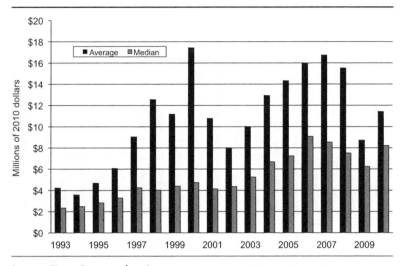

Sources: ExecuComp, author data.

Figures 3 and 4 present the analogous figures for actual, or realized, CEO pay. Recall that this measure includes exercised options issued in the past. Figure 3 shows that average actual pay also peaked in 2000, dipped by more than 50 percent by 2002, rebounded close to 2000 levels by 2007, dipped markedly again in 2009, and rebounded somewhat in 2010. Average pay in 2010, at $11.6 million, is 35 percent below its peak in 2000.

Median CEO pay has continued to increase and peaked in 2006 at a value of just over $8 million. The increase in the median is the result of the increased use of restricted stock rather than stock options. Figure 4 shows a similar pattern for average and median realized pay relative to median household income. The average and median S&P 500 CEO realized, respectively, 234 and 165 times the median household in 2010.

3.2 Non–S&P 500 CEOs

Figure 5 presents average and median estimated pay for the CEOs of companies in the ExecuComp database that are not in the

Figure 4
Average and Median Total Pay of S&P 500 CEOs
Relative to Median Household Income, 1993–2010 (realized)

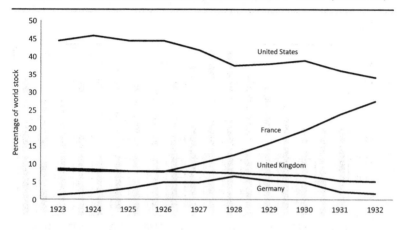

Sources: ExecuComp, Census accounts.

S&P 500. Figure 6 compares the average and estimated pay for these CEOs to the income of the median household.

Figure 5 shows that pay for these CEOs, like those in the S&P 500, increased in the 1990s and declined in the 2000s. The ups and downs, however, were smaller in magnitude than those for the S&P 500. Overall, from 1993 to 2010, average pay increased by 54 percent for non–S&P 500 CEOs compared to 150 percent for S&P 500 CEOs. Just as for S&P 500 CEOs, average pay levels today for non–S&P 500 CEOs are roughly equal to those in 1997 and 1998.

Figure 6 shows that average estimated pay of non–S&P 500 CEOs was 50 times greater than median household income in 1993, 70 times greater in 1997, and 90 times greater in 2001, before it fell back to roughly 70 times greater as of 2010.

Figure 7 reports the average and median realized pay of non–S&P 500 CEOs. Average realized pay grew through 2005, dipped markedly through 2009, and rebounded somewhat in 2010. Average pay

Figure 5
Average and Median Total Pay of Non-S&P 500 CEOs,
1993–2010 (estimated)

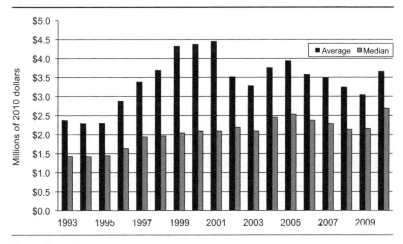

Source: ExecuComp.

Figure 6
Average and Median Total Pay of Non-S&P 500 CEOs
Relative to Median Household Income, 1993–2010 (estimated)

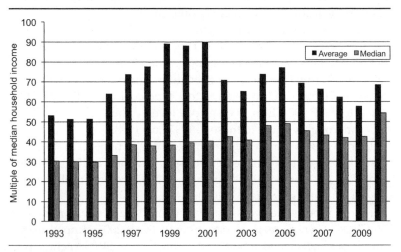

Sources: ExecuComp, Census accounts.

Figure 7
Average and Median Total Pay of Non-S&P 500 CEOs,
1993–2010 (realized)

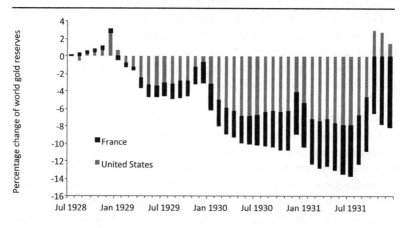

Source: ExecuComp.

in 2010, at $4.0 million, is still 20 percent below its peak in 2005 and is roughly one-third of realized pay for S&P 500 CEOs.

Overall, then, these figures show that estimated CEO pay—the pay that boards expected to pay their CEOs—peaked in 2000–2001, both for S&P 500 and non–S&P 500 CEOs. Since then, average estimated CEO pay has declined, returning to roughly the level it was in 1997 and 1998.

Nevertheless, some outliers on estimated pay still seem consistent with managerial power. In 2010, eight CEOs earned more than $30 million; three earned more than $50 million. Interestingly, those three—the CEOs of CBS, Oracle, and Viacom—are controlled by their large shareholders, Sumner Redstone (CBS and Viacom), and Larry Ellison (Oracle).

4. HOW DOES CEO PAY COMPARE TO THAT OF OTHER HIGHLY PAID PEOPLE?

Although estimated CEO pay has declined in the last 10 years, it is clear that CEOs are highly paid and have done very well since the early 1990s. The important question is why they have done so well. Are the high pay levels due to the managerial power of CEOs over their boards? Are those pay levels driven by a competitive market for talent? Or have other factors been important?

Gabaix and Landier (2008) argue that market forces explain the increases in CEO pay. In a simple competitive model, they show that as firms get bigger, CEOs will get paid more. A talented CEO creates more value as a firm becomes larger. In a competitive market, CEO pay will be bid up as firms become larger. Larger average firm size increases the returns to hiring a more productive CEO. They find empirically that increases in CEO pay since 1980 can be fully attributed to the increase in large company market values.

Frydman and Saks (2010) studied top executive pay from the 1930s to 2005. They, too, conclude that the evidence is not consistent with the managerial power/rent extraction story. Yet their results call into question the story in Gabaix and Landier because CEO pay did not increase with firm market value before 1970 and because changes in firm size explain less of the variation in changes in compensation.

Gabaix and Landier, Frydman and Saks, and Murphy and Zábojník (2008) focus on the market for top executives of public companies. But the same individuals can also become executives at private companies, become (or remain) consultants, and—earlier in their careers—become lawyers, investment bankers, and investors. In a competitive market for talent, similarly talented individuals should have done as well as CEOs over the last 20 or 30 years.

That is indeed what has occurred. Piketty and Saez (2003 and 2006) show that the share of pretax income earned by very high earners—the top 1 percent or top 0.1 percent—has increased markedly over the last 30 years. Figures 8 and 9 reproduce the income share—as expressed in adjusted gross income (AGI)—for the top 0.1 percent of earners from 1914 to 2010, and the more recent period from 1989 to 2010, respectively. The pattern in Figure 9 shows roughly the same patterns as those for CEO pay in Figures 1, 3, 5, and 7.

In Kaplan and Rauh (2010), Josh Rauh and I compare how well off CEOs and top executives were in 2004 (the most recent year with good data available when we wrote the paper) compared to 1994 (the first year in which good data were available) relative to other top earners. Figure 10 updates this analysis by comparing the average estimated pay of S&P 500 CEOs to the average pay of U.S. taxpayers in the

Figure 8
Income Share (AGI) of Top 0.1% of U.S. Taxpayers, 1913–2010

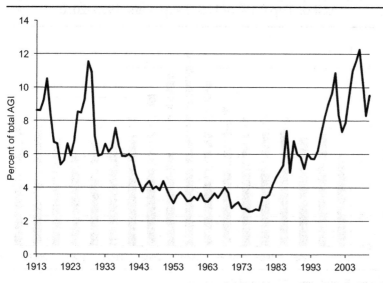

Source: Piketty and Saez (2010).

Figure 9
Income Share (AGI) of Top 0.1% of U.S. Taxpayers, 1989–2010

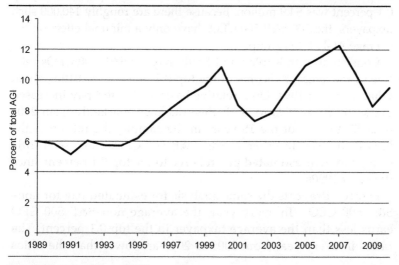

Source: Piketty and Saez (2010).

Figure 10
Average Pay (Estimated) of S&P 500 CEOs Relative to Average
AGI of Top 0.1% of U.S. Taxpayers, 1993–2010

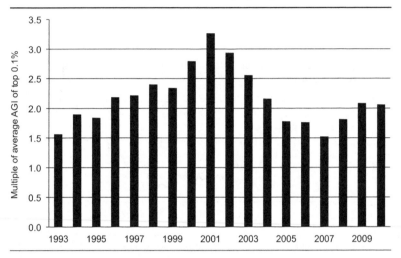

Sources: ExecuComp, Piketty and Saez (2010).

top 0.1 percent from 1993 to 2010. In 2010, the AGI cutoff for the top 0.1 percent was $1.5 million; the average AGI for taxpayers in the top 0.1 percent was $4.9 million. Because there are roughly 140,000 such taxpayers, the 500 S&P 500 CEOs have only a minimal effect on the average AGI of this group.

Consistent with Kaplan and Rauh, pay for S&P 500 CEOs relative to the average income of the top 0.1 percent in 2010 is about what it was in 1994. On a relative basis, estimated pay increased markedly from 1993 to 2001, then declined markedly from 2001 to 2007. In fact, of the 18 years in the sample, the ratio was the lowest in 2007. In other words, S&P 500 CEOs have seen little change in their estimated pay relative to the top 0.1 percent since the early 1990s.

Figure 11 repeats the same analysis for estimated pay for non–S&P 500 CEOs. In every year, the average non–S&P 500 CEO earns less than the average taxpayer in the top 0.1 percent. The ratios in every year from 2005 to 2010 are lower than the ratios

Figure 11
Average Pay (Estimated) of Non-S&P 500 ExecuComp CEOs Relative to Average AGI of Top 0.1% of U.S. Taxpayers, 1993–2010

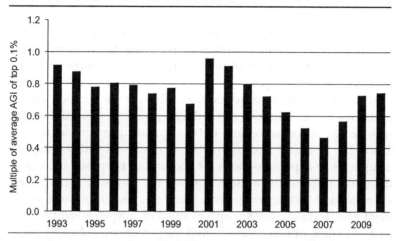

Sources: ExecuComp, Piketty and Saez (2010).

before 1998. Non–S&P 500 CEOs are worse off in their estimated pay relative to the top 0.1 percent than they were in the early and mid-1990s.

Over the last 20 years (the period in which the level of estimated CEO pay increased markedly), CEO pay relative to the top 0.1 percent has remained relatively constant or even declined. That result is consistent with a competitive market for talent. To use evidence of higher public company CEO pay as proof of managerial power or rents would require an explanation of why others in the very top income groups—not subject to managerial power effects—have seen a similar growth in pay.

The greater puzzle in these figures is why estimated CEO pay increased so much at S&P 500 firms from 1993 to 2001 and declined so much from 2001 to 2007, both in real terms and relative to the top 0.1 percent of U.S. taxpayers. Murphy (forthcoming) rejects the simple managerial-power explanation for these patterns for several reasons. First, there is no evidence that boards have become weaker over time. In fact, most evidence suggests the opposite. Second, the largest increases in pay go to CEOs hired externally, from outside the company. Those CEOs are hired in arm's-length negotiations with boards over whom they have no power initially. Third, as we saw above, the price of alternative talent increased significantly.

Instead, Murphy (2012) attributes the large run-up in CEO pay (particularly option-based pay) in the 1990s not to managerial power, but to four different forces: First, boards responded to increased shareholder pressure for equity-based pay. Second, Bill Clinton and Congress passed Section 162(m) of the tax code, which permitted public companies to deduct top executive pay if that pay was tied to performance, and options qualified for the deduction. Third, the Financial Accounting Standards Board did not require companies to expense options for accounting purposes as long as the strike price of the options equaled the company's grant date share price. Most option grants, therefore, had no income statement cost, so many boards undervalued or misperceived the true cost of issuing options. Fourth, that misperception led many companies to award the same *number* of options each year rather than options with the same *value*. As stock prices increased markedly in the 1990s, the value of those options increased markedly as well. These four forces fueled the run-up. It reversed after 2000 because of a backlash from the Internet bust, because companies increasingly expensed options (and were required to do so by 2006), and because of stricter rules on option plans from the New York Stock Exchange and NASDAQ. I am sympathetic to Murphy's analysis, particularly for the S&P 500 CEOs.

Figures 12 and 13 report the analogous analyses for realized pay. Since 1997, realized pay of S&P 500 CEOs has been stable at 2.0 to 2.5 times the average pay of the top 0.1 percent. From 1993 to 1996, realized pay was somewhat lower, at roughly 1.75 times. At the same time, the average pay of non–S&P 500 CEOs has varied from 0.6 to 0.8 times the average pay of the top 0.1 percent since 1994, with no obvious trend. The ratio was relatively low in 2007 and 2008 at roughly 0.6 and relatively high in 2010 at roughly 0.8. Overall, the ratios have remained relatively stable for both sets of CEOs. And, again, there is little evidence that the CEOs have been particularly better off than others in the top 0.1 percent.

Figure 12
Average Pay (Realized) of S&P 500 CEOs Relative to Average AGI of Top 0.1% of U.S. Taxpayers, 1993–2010

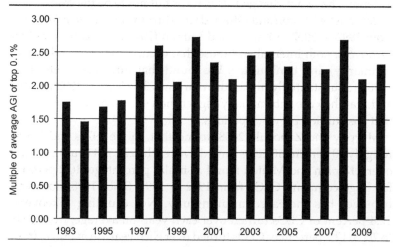

Sources: ExecuComp, Piketty and Saez (2010).

Figure 13
Average Pay (Realized) of Non-S&P 500 ExecuComp CEOs Relative to Average AGI of Top 0.1% of Taxpayers, 1993–2010

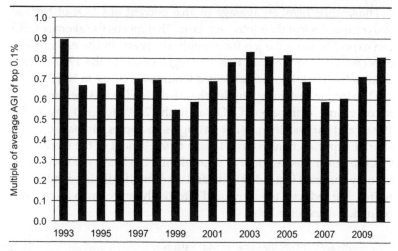

Sources: ExecuComp, Piketty and Saez (2010).

5.   WHAT HAS HAPPENED TO CEO TURNOVER?

The previous analyses look at how CEO pay has changed over time. They implicitly assume that other aspects of the CEO job, such as tenure, have not changed. This turns out not to be the case.

Bernadette Minton and I studied CEO turnover in *Fortune* 500 firms from 1992 to 2007 in Kaplan and Minton (2012).[7] We considered all turnovers, both internal and those that occurred through takeovers (primarily) and bankruptcy. We found that turnover levels since 1998 are substantially higher than turnover levels from 1992 to 1997, and that they are substantially higher than shown in previous work that has studied previous periods.

Murphy and Zábojník (2008) found that, in the 1970s and 1980s, roughly 10 percent of CEOs turned over each year, not counting takeovers. Kaplan and Minton found a similar percentage, 10.2 percent, for large-company CEOs from 1992 to 1997. Since 1998, however, turnover has increased meaningfully. Not counting takeovers, 12.4 percent of CEOs turned over each year, on average, from 1998 to 2003; 12.2 percent of CEOs turned over each year, on average, from 2004 to 2010. Figure 14 updates the Kaplan and Minton data through 2010 and reports it graphically.

When takeovers are included, the changes are greater. From 1992 to 1997, total CEO turnover averaged 13.0 percent; from 1998 to 2003, total turnover averaged 17.6 percent; and from 2004 to 2010, 15.8 percent.

Thus, since 1998, an average of 16.6 percent of CEOs of *Fortune* 500 companies lost their jobs each year. That means the average CEO can expect to have the job for roughly six years. In the early 1990s, expected CEO tenure was closer to eight years. In the 1970s, when there were few takeovers, expected tenure was closer to 10 years.

The decline in tenure implies that the CEO job has become riskier over time. Comparing CEO pay in the 2000s to CEO pay in the 1990s (and earlier), then, is not an apples-to-apples comparison. The shorter expected tenure offsets some of the benefit of the increase in CEO pay over this period. For example, if a CEO earns CEO-like pay for only six years instead of eight and earns markedly less if he or she retires, the reduced tenure would effectively represent a 25 percent reduction in expected pay.

---

[7] The results are virtually the same for S&P 500 firms.

Figure 14
Internal and Total Annual Turnover of *Fortune* 500 CEOs, 1992–2010

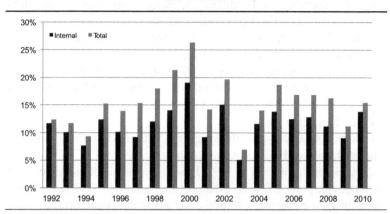

Source: Updated from Kaplan and Minton (2012).

Peters and Wagner (2012, 5) estimated this relationship explicitly. They found "a robust and significantly positive association between predicted turnover risk and CEO compensation." In their paper, a 1 percent increase in turnover risk is associated with a 10 percent increase in pay. If turnover has increased by 2 percent, then risk-adjusted pay should have increased by 20 percent.

Taking this seriously, CEO pay in 2010 in Figures 1–7 and 10–13 would need to be reduced by at least 20 percent relative to CEO pay before 1998. That would make the decline in real CEO pay and CEO pay relative to others in the top 0.1 percent even greater than described above. In other words, CEOs have done relatively worse compared to their early 1990s counterparts than the compensation figures alone would suggest.

6.   WHAT ABOUT THE LONGER TERM?

Both Frydman and Saks (2010) and Frydman and Jenter (2010) consider long-run patterns of large-company CEO pay. Frydman and Saks conclude that "the long-run trends in pay seem inconsistent with explanations related to managerial rent seeking." At the same time, they conclude that the firm scale explanation of Gabaix and

119

Landier (2008), who "predict that compensation should correlate 1-to-1 with the growth in the size of the aggregate value of firms," is unsuccessful before 1970.

For this section, like Frydman and Saks, I compared a long time series of estimated CEO pay with firm size, and I obtained results similar to theirs. I also compared that times series of estimated CEO pay with the average pay of the top 0.1 percent of U.S. taxpayers. Here the results were somewhat different. Over the long term, estimated CEO pay has moved with the pay of the top 0.1 percent. This suggests an important competitive market component for CEO pay over the long term.

To look at CEO pay over the long term, I stapled together three data sets. First, I used the ExecuComp data for S&P 500 CEOs from 1992 to 2010. Second, for 1980 to 1992, I used the means of estimated pay for large-company CEOs in Hall and Leibman (1998). The Hall and Leibman data come from roughly 400 firms that were on the *Forbes* magazine list of the largest U.S. public companies in the 1980s. Like the S&P 500 companies, these are representative of large public companies. (Hall and Leibman present estimates from 1980 to 1994.) To make them comparable, I indexed the Hall and Leibman numbers to the 1992 ExecuComp numbers. That is, I calculated 1991 pay as the 1992 ExecuComp pay changed by the percentage change in the Hall and Leibman pay numbers from 1991 to 1992. The percentage pay changes in Hall and Leibman from 1992 to 1994 of 2 percent and 21 percent are similar to the percentage pay changes in ExecuComp of 1 percent and 24 percent for those years, suggesting the sample firms are similar.

Third, for 1936 to 1980, I used the annual means of estimated pay from Frydman and Saks (2010).[8] Those data come from the 50 largest publicly traded companies in 1940, 1960, and 1990, which they followed over time. They argue that these data also are representative of a group of large companies.

The resulting series is somewhat different from Frydman and Saks, who show a larger increase in pay over time. The reason is that the average increase in CEO pay in Frydman and Saks from 1980 to 1994 data is larger (289 percent) than the average increase (209 percent) in the Hall and Leibman data; the Frydman and Saks increases also are greater than those reported by Murphy (2012) for the 1980s.

---

[8] I thank Carola Frydman for providing them.

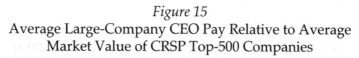

Figure 15
Average Large-Company CEO Pay Relative to Average
Market Value of CRSP Top-500 Companies

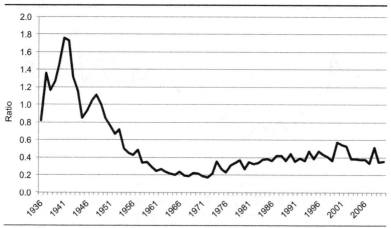

Sources: S&P 500 CEO pay for 1992–2010 are from ExecuComp; large-company CEO pay for 1980–1992 are from Hall and Leibman (1998); and large-company CEO pay for 1936–1980 are from Frydman and Saks (2010). Average market value of top-500 companies for 1936–2010 are from the Center for Research in Security Prices.

Figure 15 shows the ratio of average CEO pay to the average stock market value of the top 500 publicly traded companies according to the Center for Research in Security Prices. I report the ratio multiplied by 1,000. The figure shows that CEO pay was a much higher fraction of market value in the 1930s and 1940s than it was in the 1960s. Figure 16 shows that today the ratio is similar to its level in the late 1970s and the late 1950s. Said another way, market values increased through 1960 much more than CEO pay. The growth rates of market values exceeded pay in the 1960s, but caught up again by the late 1970s. The ratios increased modestly through 2000 and have declined since, returning to their late 1950s level. The data, then, support the Gabaix and Landier (2008) prediction about the positive relationship between firm size and CEO pay since the late 1970s, but not before.

Figure 17 shows average CEO pay in 2010 dollars and the ratio of CEO pay to the average pay of the top 0.1 percent from 1936 to 2010. Figure 18 shows only the ratio. While average pay has increased markedly in the last 30 years, the ratio of pay to the top 0.1 percent has increased by much less. The ratio increased from the mid-1980s to the

Figure 16
Average Large-Company CEO Pay Relative to Average
Market Value of CRSP Top-500 Companies, 1960–2010

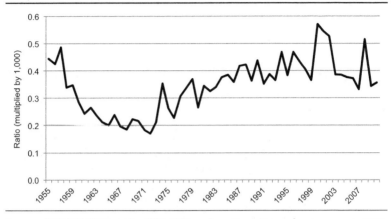

Sources: S&P 500 CEO pay for 1992–2010 are from ExecuComp; large-company CEO
pay for 1980–1992 are from Hall and Leibman (1998); and large-company CEO pay
for 1936–1980 are from Frydman and Saks (2010). Average market value of top-500
companies for 1936-2010 are from CRSP.

Figure 17
Average Large-Company CEO Pay and Ratio of Average
Large-Company CEO Pay to Average Pay of Top 0.1%

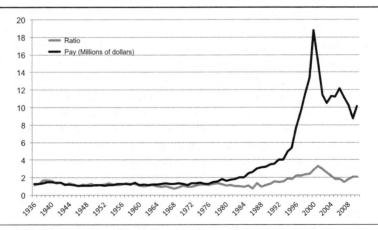

Sources: ExecuComp 1992–2010; Hall and Leibman (1998) 1980–1992; Frydman and
Saks (2010) 1936–1980; Piketty and Saez (2010).

Figure 18
Average Large-Company CEO Pay to Average AGI of
Top 0.1%, 1936–2010

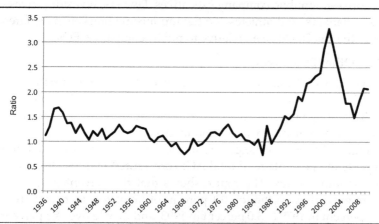

Sources: ExecuComp, Hall and Leibman (1998); Frydman and Saks (2010); Piketty and Saez (2010).

turn of the century. Since then, it has declined, although it remains above its level in the mid-1980s. Interestingly, the ratio in 2007 was lower than the ratio in the late 1930s, when dispersed shareholdings and problems of managerial power were presumably less acute than they are today. The ratio today is modestly higher than in the late 1930s.

The unanswered question is, what drove the ratio so high in the 1990s and has led to its decline since then? Murphy and Zábojník (2008) and Frydman (2007) argue that part of the increase since the 1980s can be explained by a movement toward CEOs with more general skills and by a more competitive labor market. In particular, Murphy and Zábojník attribute the increase in executive pay to the increased prevalence of hiring CEOs from outside the firm.

Nevertheless, Murphy (2012) doubts that such changes can explain the increase in pay levels in the late 1990s. As already mentioned, government policies and regulations likely played an important role. In addition, Holmstrom and Kaplan (2001) and Murphy (2012) both suggest that the relatively low pay of CEOs at the start of the 1980s was suboptimal.

In summary, taken together, Figures 15–18 suggest that a combination of firm scale and the market for talent are associated with a meaningful amount of the movement of large-company CEO pay over time.

7. HOW DO CEOs COMPARE TO OTHER HIGHLY PAID GROUPS?

In this section, I present more detailed evidence on how other groups—nonpublic company executives, lawyers, investors, investment bankers, and athletes—in the top income brackets have fared over the last 20–30 years relative to public company CEOs.

7.1 Other Executives

Bakija, Cole, and Heim (2012) studied IRS tax return data for a number of years between 1979 and 2005. They were able to distinguish among taxpayers who were employed as business executives, financial executives, lawyers, and in medicine.

Figure 19 looks at taxpayers in the top 0.1 percent of AGI and reports the percentage of total AGI contributed by those taxpayers in the four groups. The figure shows that the percentage of AGI from executives in the top 0.1 percent of taxpayers increased from 1.5 percent in 1979 to 3.0 percent in 1993, and then to over 4.5 percent in 2005. Taxpayers in finance increased from 0.4 percent in 1979, to 0.9 percent in 1993, to over 2.0 percent in 2005. Those increases

Figure 19
Percent of Total Income (AGI) for Various Occupation Groups in the Top 0.1% of Taxpayers

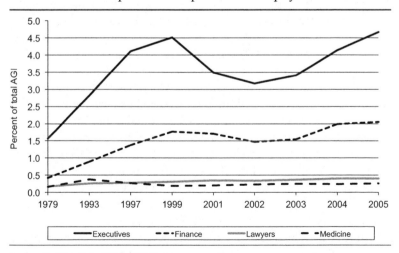

Source: Bakija, Cole, Heim (2012).

compare to income shares of all top-0.1 percent taxpayers of 3.4 percent in 1979, to 5.7 percent in 1993, to 11.0 percent in 2005. The share of the top 0.1 percent, then, increased more than three times. Executives increased their shares by roughly the same three times while taxpayers in finance increased their share by roughly five times. The larger relative increase in finance is consistent with the results and arguments in Kaplan and Rauh (2010) and Philippon and Reshef (2008) that financial executives did particularly well over this period.

Bakija, Cole, and Heim (2012) cannot identify whether the executives in their sample work for private or public companies, or whether the taxpayers are CEOs or not. They try to distinguish between public and private company CEOs by comparing executives who receive the majority of their income in salary and wages with those who receive the majority of their income from self-employment, partnership, and S-corporation-related income, not salary and wages. They argue that the former are more likely to include public company executives while the latter are more likely to include executives of closely held businesses. Bakija, Cole, and Heim (2012) also distinguish among executives, managers, and supervisors. In Figure 20, I combine those three groups. The conclusions and patterns are similar if I look only at executives.

Figure 20 is the key graph from the Bakija, Cole, and Heim (2012) data. It indicates that the pay of executives of closely held businesses increased more than the pay of salaried executives from 1979 to 1993, and again from 1993 to 2005. Figure 21 shows that executives of closely held firms accounted for roughly 22 percent of the top 0.1 percent in 2005, up from 18 percent in 1993 and 9 percent in 1979. At the same time, salaried executives made up 20 percent of the top 0.1 percent in 2005, down from 28 percent in 1993 and 38 percent in 1979.

Public company executives—who are presumably more subject to problems of managerial power—saw their pay and relative standing increase less over this period than executives of closely held companies that are, by definition, controlled by large shareholders or the executives, and are subject to limited agency problems. This is notable because many of the salaried and closely held company executives likely come from the same general executive pool and, presumably, can move between public company and private company employment. Again, using evidence of higher public company

Figure 20
Percent of Total Income (AGI) Earned by Executives, Managers, and Supervisors (Combined) in Top 0.1% of Taxpayers

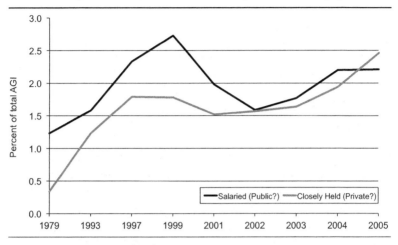

Source: Bakija, Cole, Heim (2012).

Figure 21
Percent of Executives, Managers, and Supervisors (Combined) in Top 0.1% of Taxpayers

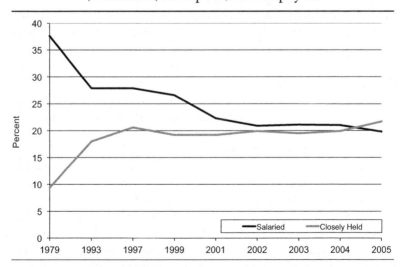

Source: Bakija, Cole, Heim (2012).

executive pay as inherent evidence of capture or managerial power requires an explanation of why private company executives and the other professional groups have had similar or higher growth in pay where managerial power concerns are largely absent.

7.2 Lawyers

Lawyers at top law firms are another useful comparison group for CEOs. Much of the work these lawyers perform is for corporate clients. Because the law firms are partnerships and their fees are negotiated in an arm's-length manner with clients, partner pay at such firms is arguably market-based and not subject to managerial power concerns. It can also be argued that top lawyers are drawn from a similar undergraduate pool as top public company executives. In addition, it is useful to note that the general counsels of large public companies are often former law partners. Accordingly, there is some overlap in the market for talent between top executives and top lawyers.

Figure 22 reports average profit per partner at the 50 top law firms from *American Lawyer* magazine surveys from 1994 to 2010. This

Figure 22
Average Profit Per Partner at Top 50 Law Firms, 1994–2010

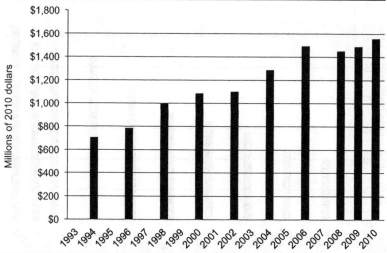

Source: *American Lawyer*, various years.

calculation measures the total partner profits at all 50 firms divided by the total number of partners. (The average of the profits per partner at each firm is slightly higher.) The average profit per partner provides an estimate of the average partner's AGI earned from employment at his or her law firm. The average profit per partner increased from $0.7 million in 1994 to almost $1.6 million in 2010 (in 2010 dollars). Figure 23 shows that the average profit per partner increased from 10 times median household income to 30 times over this period. Figure 24 shows the average partner's income increased from roughly one-quarter to between 0.30 and 0.35 of the average income of the top 0.1 percent of taxpayers. Figure 25 shows that estimated pay of the average S&P 500 CEO was roughly six times that of the average law partner in 1994 and remains at that level today after diverging in the late 1990s. Finally, Figure 26 shows that estimated pay of non–S&P 500 CEOs has declined from three times the average top-50 law firm partner to two times. In other words, the average S&P 500 CEO and the average top-50 law firm partner have

Figure 23
Average Profit Per Partner at Top 50 Law Firms Relative to Median Household Income, 1994–2010

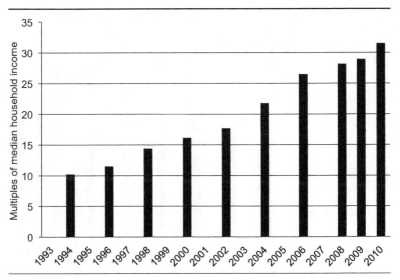

Sources: *American Lawyer*, Census.

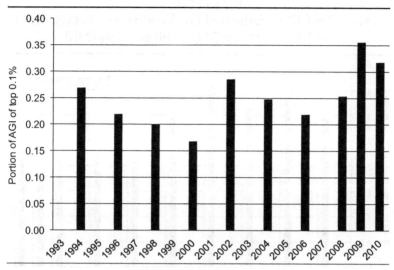

Figure 24
Average Profit Per Partner at Top 50 Law Firms Relative to
Average AGI of Top 0.1%, 1994–2010

Sources: *American Lawyer*, Piketty and Saez (2010).

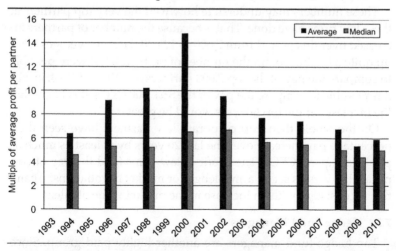

Figure 25
S&P 500 CEO Pay (Estimated) Relative to Average Profit Per
Partner at Top 50 Law Firms, 1994–2010

Sources: ExecuComp, *American Lawyer*.

Figure 26
Non-S&P 500 CEO Estimated Pay Relative to Average Profit
Per Partner at Top 50 Law Firms, 1994–2010

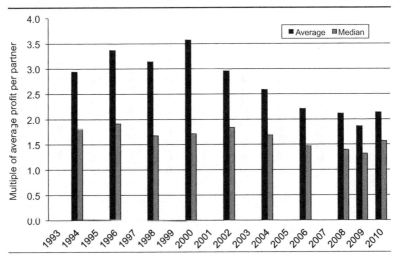

Sources: ExecuComp, *American Lawyer.*

done roughly as well over the last 20 years. The lawyers have done relatively better than non–S&P 500 CEOs.

These numbers may understate how well the very top partners at these law firms have done. That is because the number of partners increased over this period from 7,000 to 12,000 (i.e., the averages went up quite a bit, but so did the number of partners). If it were possible to compare the pay of the top 7,000 partners in 2010 and 1994, just as it is possible to compare the pay of the S&P 500 CEOs, it is likely that the increase for the top lawyers would be greater.

On the whole then, top corporate law partners have seen their percentage pay increase over the last 20 years by at least as much as public company CEOs. The profit of law firms (and the pay of corporate lawyers) is set by arm's-length or market negotiations. Again, this is consistent with an increase in the market value of talent.

7.3 Hedge Fund Managers

Top hedge fund managers are another highly paid group. Since 2001, *Absolute Return + Alpha (AR)* magazine has published an annual

Figure 27
Average Pay of Top 25 Hedge Fund Managers, 2001–2011

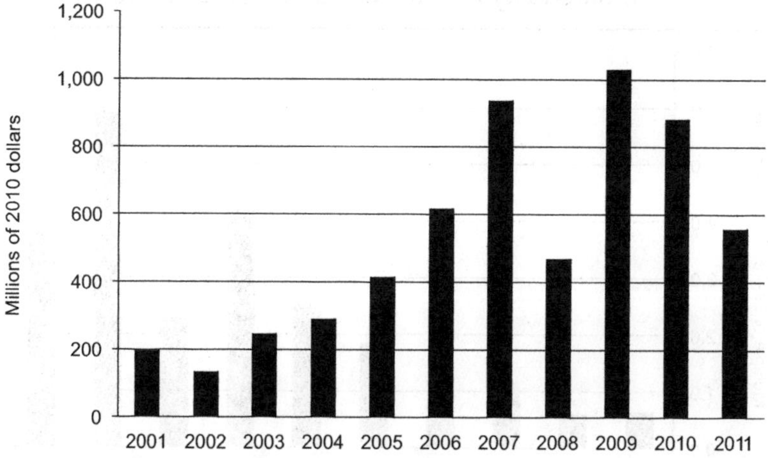

Source: *Absolute Return + Alpha.*

"Rich List" of the 25 highest paid hedge fund managers. *AR* estimates the annual income of these managers from fees and their capital invested in their funds. As a result, *AR* overstates the income of these managers attributable to their employment per se, as separate from their investment income. Nevertheless, the results are striking.

Figure 27 reports the average income of these hedge fund managers (in millions of 2010 dollars). The average peaked at over $1 billion in 2007 and was as low as $134 million in 2002. These numbers are much higher than the averages for S&P 500 CEOs.

Figure 28 puts this into perspective. It compares the combined incomes of the 25 highest paid hedge fund managers to the combined estimated pay of the S&P 500 CEOs from 2001 to 2011. From 2001 to 2004, the ratio was roughly 1.0, implying that 25 hedge fund managers earned roughly as much as S&P 500 CEOs. Since 2004, however, the ratio has grown substantially. In 2010, the 25 hedge fund managers earned roughly four times as much as the S&P 500 CEOs. In other words, hedge fund managers appear to have done considerably better than CEOs over this period.

131

Figure 28

Total Pay of Top 25 Hedge Fund Managers Relative to Total
Estimated Pay of 500 S&P 500 CEOs, 2001–10

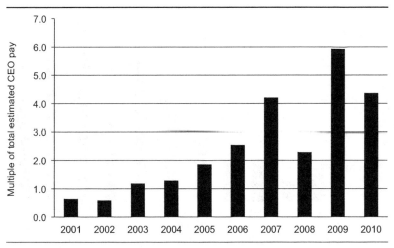

Sources: ExecuComp, *Absolute Return + Alpha.*

Consistent with these figures, the *Forbes* magazine list of the 400 wealthiest Americans for 2011 (the most recent at the time this paper was written) includes at least 26 hedge fund managers, with 10 among the top 100 richest Americans. At the same time, the list does not include one public company CEO who earned most of his or her equity when the company was public. Two non-founder public company CEOs are among the top 100—Steve Ballmer of Microsoft and Eric Schmidt, formerly of Google—but both received most of their equity before their companies went public.

7.4 Private Equity Investors

Kaplan and Rauh (2010) document a large increase in fees to private equity (PE) and venture capital (VC) investors through 2005. Since 2005, the assets under management in private equity have increased substantially.

Figures 29 and 30 calculate the fees and document their growth in two ways. Both figures assume private equity and venture capital investors earn fees on capital raised over a recent seven-year period.

Figure 29
Estimated Fees of U.S. Private Equity and Venture Capital
Funds Using Annual Returns

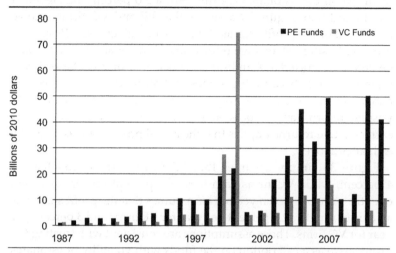

Sources: *Private Equity Analyst*, Cambridge Associates, Steven Kaplan.

Figure 30
Estimated Fees of U.S. Private Equity and Venture Capital
Funds (assuming 4% and 5% of assets under management)

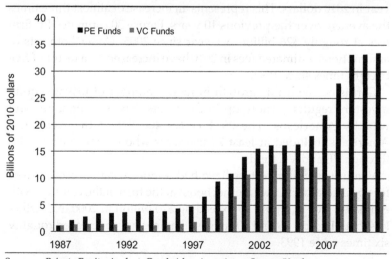

Sources: *Private Equity Analyst*, Cambridge Associates, Steven Kaplan.

Capital raised or committed is obtained from *Private Equity Analyst* newsletter.

Figure 29 assumes that the PE firms earn a 1.5 percent management fee on that capital; VC firms earn a 2.0 percent management fee. In addition, Figure 29 assumes that PE and VC firms receive 20 percent of the profits earned by funds in a given year. Profits are estimated using the average return earned by PE and VC funds in a given year, reported by Cambridge Associates. This calculation likely understates fees because it assumes that all funds earn the average annual return. Because the 20 percent profit share is applied only to positive returns, any dispersion across funds such that some funds earn negative returns implies that the actual profit share exceeds the estimates above.

Figure 30 simply assumes that PE firms earn overall fees of 4 percent, while VC firms earn fees of 5 percent on capital raised over the previous seven years. This assumes that the profit share has a value of roughly 2.5 percent per year for PE firms and 3 percent per year for VC firms. Those assumptions are consistent with treating the profit share as a call option on the funds with volatility of estimates 28 percent and 35 percent, respectively, for PE and VC funds. The 4 percent and 5 percent assumptions also are consistent with the fee estimates in Metrick and Yasuda (2010).

Figure 29 shows that fees to PE firms have increased substantially over time. Since 2005, they have averaged roughly $34 billion per year in 2010 dollars. This represents an increase of almost three times the average over the previous 10 years. Figure 30 estimates PE firm fees at roughly $26 billion per year since 2005. Under both sets of assumptions, estimated fees in 2010 have increased by a factor of five to eight times since 1993.

Consistent with this growth in fees, a number of private equity investors regularly show up in the *Forbes* lists of billionaires and wealthy Americans. The 2011 *Forbes* 400 list of the wealthiest Americans included at least 25 members who earned their wealth through PE and VC funds.

Venture capital investors have had a more volatile record. Their fees peaked around the Internet boom at the turn of the century, with estimated fees in Figure 29 exceeding $70 billion in 2000. Nevertheless, both Figures 29 and 30 suggest that fees have increased roughly six times since 1993.

7.5   Athletes

Kaplan and Rauh also compare CEO pay to that for professional athletes in baseball, basketball, and football in 1995 and 2004. I extend that analysis by looking at the average pay of the top 25 most highly paid athletes in those sports.

Figure 31 reports those averages for baseball, basketball, and football in every other year from 1993 to 2011. Pay at the top has increased markedly for the athletes since 1993, with baseball, basketball, and football players earning, respectively, 2.5, 3.3, and 5.8 times as much in 2009 as in 1993.

Figure 32 gives average estimated pay for S&P 500 CEOs relative to the average pay of the athletes. The figure shows that in 2009, compared to 1993, the S&P 500 CEOs have done roughly as well as the top baseball players, but not as well as the top basketball and football players.

7.6   Summary

The point of these comparisons is to confirm that while public company CEOs earn a great deal, they are not unique. Other groups with

Figure 31
Average Top 25 Salaries in Professional Baseball, Basketball, and Football

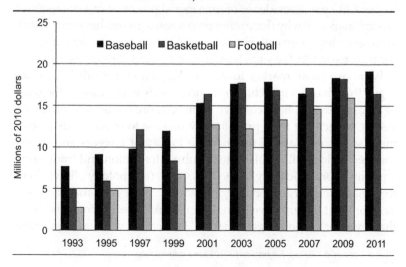

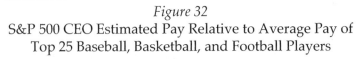

Figure 32
S&P 500 CEO Estimated Pay Relative to Average Pay of
Top 25 Baseball, Basketball, and Football Players

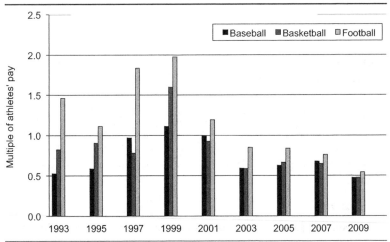

similar backgrounds—private company executives, corporate lawyers, hedge fund investors, private equity investors, and others—have seen significant pay increases where there is a competitive market for talent and managerial power problems are absent. Again, to use evidence of higher CEO pay as evidence of managerial power or capture requires an explanation of why these other professional groups have had a similar or even higher growth in pay. More likely, a meaningful portion of the increase in CEO pay has been driven by market forces as well.

What are those market forces? In Kaplan and Rauh (2010), we argue that changes in technology, along with an increase in the scale of enterprises and finance, have allowed more talented or fortunate people to increase their productivity relative to others. This assessment seems relevant to the increase in pay of lawyers and investors (technology allows them to acquire information and trade large amounts more efficiently) as well as CEOs (technology allows them to manage very large global organizations). It suggests that increases in incomes at the top have been driven more by technology and scale than by poor corporate governance.[9] Under this view, as firms have

---

[9] See Parker and Vissing-Jorgensen (2010) for a concurring view.

become more valuable and technology increasingly has allowed CEOs to affect that value, boards have responded by spending more to attract and motivate talent.

8.   WHAT DO BOARDS DO? ARE THEY CONTROLLED BY THEIR CEOs?

According to the managerial power story, managers control their boards and the boards are too friendly to management: boards do not pay for performance and boards do not fire CEOs for poor performance. This section considers the evidence for this.

8.1   Are CEOs Paid for Performance?

Critics contend that CEOs are not paid for good stock performance. For example, *New York Times* columnist Gretchen Morgenson recently wrote, "Many corporate boards talk a good line about paying for performance. Then they turn around and award fat paychecks to chief executives who, by many measures, don't deserve them."[10]

On average, that is not the case. In some cases, the critics confuse estimated pay—what the boards give to the CEOs as estimated pay—and realized pay. The key question is whether CEOs who perform better earn more in realized pay.

For each year from 1999 to 2004, Kaplan and Rauh (2010) took all the firms in the ExecuComp database and sorted them into five groups based on size (assets). We did this because it is well established that pay is tied to firm size: bigger firms pay more. Within each size group for each year, we sorted the CEOs into five groups based on how much compensation they actually realized. We then looked at how the stocks of each group performed relative to their industry over the previous three years. (The results are qualitatively and statistically identical if we use one year or five years.)

Figure 33 presents the results. Realized compensation is highly related to firm stock performance. Firms with CEOs in the top quintile of actual pay are the top-performing quintile relative to their industries in every size group. Firms with CEOs in the bottom quintile of actual pay are the worst-performing quintile relative to their industries in every size group. And the magnitudes of the performance differences are large. These calculations understate actual

---

[10] Gretchen Morgenson. "A Rich Game of Thrones: At Last, Signs that Shareholders Are Making Their Voices Heard." *New York Times*. April 8, 2012.

Figure 33
Three-Year Firm Performance Relative to Value-Weighted
Industry, by Quintiles, CEOs Only

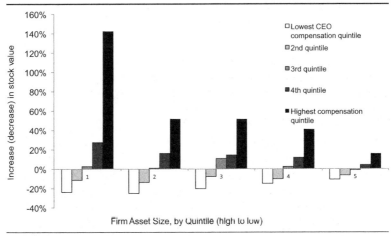

pay for performance because they value restricted stock at grant-date values. In reality, executives do not get to sell their stock at those values. At a minimum, they have to wait several years until the restricted stock vests. As a result, the values actually realized will be further tied to stock performance.

Figure 34 graphs the level of the S&P 500 index against average realized CEO pay for S&P 500 CEOs. As with the cross-section, there is a strong relationship between realized pay and stock performance in the time series.

Similarly, Frydman and Saks (2010) studied the correlation between executives' wealth and firm performance. They found that CEO wealth has been strongly tied to firm performance since the 1930s and that the relationship "strengthened considerably" after the mid-1980s.

The evidence, thus, supports the belief that realized CEO pay and CEO wealth are strongly tied to firm performance. In their surveys, Frydman and Jenter (2010) and Murphy (2012) reach similar conclusions. They calculate an "equity at stake" that measures the change in CEO wealth from a 1 percent change in stock price. Murphy reports that the equity at stake for the median S&P 500 CEO is almost $600,000 in 2010, and has been at that level or higher in all but one

Figure 34
Average Realized Pay of S&P 500 CEOs vs. S&P 500 Index,
1993–2010

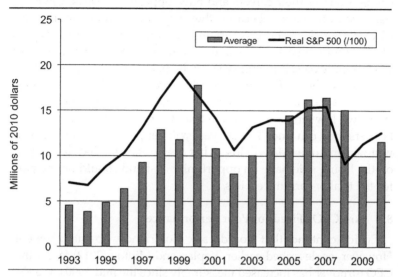

Sources: ExecuComp, Steven Kaplan.

year since 1998. Frydman and Jenter conclude that the "long run evidence shows that compensation arrangements have served to tie the wealth of managers to firm performance—and perhaps to align Managers' with shareholders' interests—for most of the twentieth century." Murphy also reports that CEOs have a large amount of wealth tied to firm performance.

The more difficult question is how much pay-for-performance is optimal and whether the current practices can become more efficient. Some argue that pay-for-performance should be increased, while others argue that pay-for-performance incentives—particularly in financial services—should be lower.

Pay-for-performance is also criticized because pay is based on absolute or actual performance rather than performance relative to a firm's industry.[11] In other words, CEOs and executives are paid to some extent for general economic conditions or luck.

---

[11] For example, see Bebchuk and Fried (2006) and Bertrand and Mullainathan (2001).

Some critics also point out that CEOs of large companies who do not perform well are still paid a great deal. This, too, is complicated. CEOs of S&P 500 companies, almost by definition, have been very successful over their careers and have opportunity costs. CEOs are paid well on average because they have other opportunities; the CEO job is riskier and less certain than in the past; and the typical S&P 500 company is a large and complicated entity with more than 20,000 employees. But while CEOs who perform poorly are paid less than CEOs who perform well, poorly performing CEOs are still paid well relative to the average worker or household. As an analogy, consider two lawyers in a corporate trial. Companies will hire the best lawyers they can find. The lawyers will get paid well. Yet, one side will win and one side will lose. That does not mean that the lawyers on the losing side have no opportunity cost and should not be paid for the trial or for future trials.

8.2   Are CEOs Fired for Poor Performance?

Critics contend that boards are too friendly to management. However, as described earlier, Kaplan and Minton (2012) found that CEO turnover has increased measurably since the mid-1990s. We also considered how that turnover varies with firm performance and found that turnover is significantly higher when firm performance is poor.

We divided firm performance into performance of the firm's industry and performance relative to the industry. We found that board-driven CEO turnover is strongly related to both. CEOs are more likely to lose their job when their firms perform poorly relative to the industry and when their industries perform poorly. The relationships are meaningful—and stronger from 1997 onward, suggesting that CEO incentives have become more linked to performance over time, not less.

The Kaplan and Minton results suggest that since 1998, annual CEO turnover is higher than at any time since 1970. The job is riskier: turnover initiated by the board is significantly related to industry stock performance and firm stock performance relative to the industry. That is, CEOs face significant performance pressure.

Jenter and Llewellen (2010) present additional evidence consistent with this conclusion. They looked at CEO turnover in the 1,600–plus firms in the ExecuComp database from 1992 to 2004. They found "that boards aggressively fire CEOs for poor performance, and that the turnover-performance sensitivity increases substantially with board

Figure 35
Five-Year CEO Turnover by Firm Performance Quintile

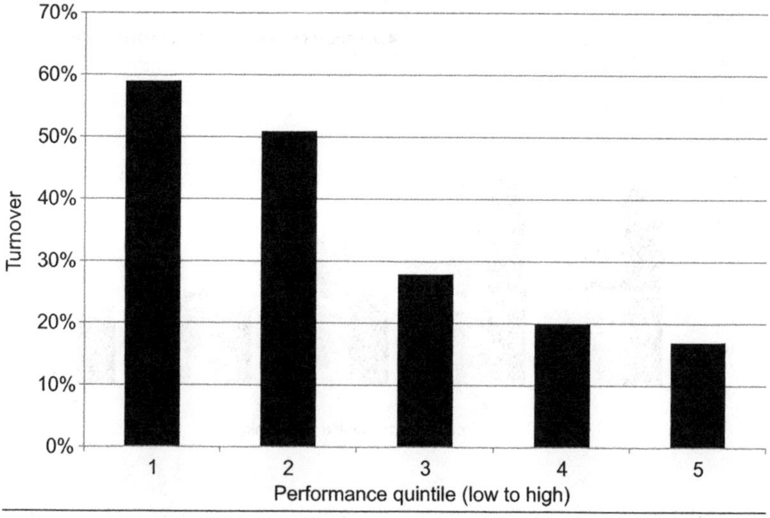

Source: Jenter and Lewellen (2010).

quality." In the first five years of tenure, CEOs who perform in the bottom quintile are 42 percent more likely to depart than CEOs in the top quintile. That spread increases to more than 70 percentage points for firms with high quality boards." (Higher quality boards have more independent directors and more director stock ownership.) Jenter and Llewellen's results are shown graphically in Figures 35 and 36.

As with pay-for-performance, the more difficult question is whether these differential departure rates are optimal and whether the current practices can become more efficient. See Taylor (2010) for an attempt at estimating this.

9. WHAT DO SHAREHOLDERS THINK?

It would be useful to know what shareholders think of all this. Fortunately, the Dodd-Frank Wall Street Reform and Consumer Protection Act of 2010 mandated that all firms with more than $75 million in publicly traded stock hold an advisory (i.e., nonbinding) shareholder vote on the compensation of the top five executives. These votes are known as say-on-pay votes. The law went into effect for proxy

Figure 36
Five-Year CEO Turnover by Firm Performance Quintile

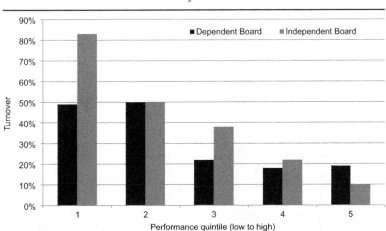

votes in 2011. According to Thomas, Palmiter, and Cotter (2011), the legislative supporters of the provision believed that by increasing shareholder power, the say-on-pay vote would reduce the CEO pay spiral and link pay to performance. This is more or less the view of those who take the managerial power position that CEOs have captured the pay process. Under the alternative view—pay levels and pay-for-performance are largely determined in a competitive market for talent—say-on-pay votes would be unnecessary. The say-on-pay votes, therefore, set up a useful test of the two views.

The results of these votes in 2011 overwhelmingly favored existing pay policies. Equilar (2011) reported that only 38 of 2,252 companies (less than 2 percent) received less than a majority of favorable votes. Only 165 (less than 8 percent) received a favorable vote under 70 percent of the voting shareholders.[12] At the same time, 1,654 companies (more than 73 percent) received a favorable vote of more than 90 percent of the voting shareholders. The results were similar at larger companies, with pay policies receiving shareholder approval at more than 98 percent of S&P 500 companies. Figures 37 and 38 report these results graphically.

---

[12] Mishra (2012) reports that 182 of 2,500 firms, or 7.3 percent, received a favorable vote of less than 70 percent.

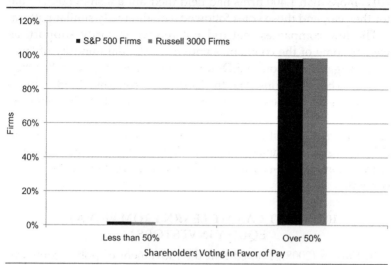

Figure 37
Say-On-Pay Favorable Votes in 2011

Source: Equilar.

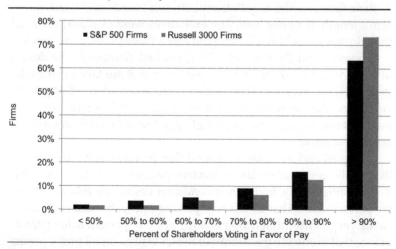

Figure 38
Say-On-Pay Favorable Votes, 2011

Source: Equilar.

Those levels of approval do not appear to be a one-year phenomenon. At the time this paper was written, in the summer of 2012, more than 1,400 firms had held their annual shareholder vote for the year, and those votes followed a qualitatively similar pattern.

The few companies that did not receive majority support, as well as some of the companies with a substantial minority of "no" votes, suggest that some CEOs do exert managerial power. But they appear to be exceptions. And the "no" votes from shareholders highlight those exceptions and put pressure on boards to fix them. At the same time, the positive shareholder votes for most companies seem inconsistent with the view that CEO and top executive pay are driven largely by managerial power. Rather, the votes are consistent with a more market-based view of top executive pay for the typical company.

10. WHAT CAN WE LEARN FROM PRIVATE EQUITY INVESTORS?

In Kaplan (2008), I noted that the movement of public company CEOs to work for private equity firms and private equity–funded companies was consistent with a competitive market for executives. Private equity investors are strongly motivated to make profits. Any extra compensation to a CEO reduces the profit of a private equity investor. In addition, private equity investors control the boards of their firms, so the negotiations between boards and CEOs are at arm's length. If public company executives were overpaid for what they do, they would not be likely to leave those public companies.

Cronqvist and Fahlenbrach (2011) studied changes in the design of CEO contracts for publicly traded firms that are taken private by private equity investors. They did not find any evidence that private equity sponsors reduce base salaries, bonuses, and perquisites. They interpret this as suggesting that CEO pay levels in public companies are not excessive.

Cronqvist and Fahlenbrach found that private equity investors—like public companies—use subjective performance evaluation and time-vesting equity, and do not condition vesting on relative industry performance. That is, CEOs of private equity–funded companies (with very concentrated ownership) are compensated for performance that is outside the control of the CEO (e.g., an oil firm's profits increase owing to an increase in the price of oil or to another positive industry shock). This is worth mentioning, given the criticism mentioned earlier that public company executives are paid for luck. If relative performance evaluation were meaningfully more efficient, we would expect to see private equity investors make more use of it.

At the same time, Cronqvist and Fahlenbrach found that CEO contracts make less use of earnings-based and nonfinancial measures and greater use of equity grant performance–vesting based on pre-specified performance measures, and require terminated CEOs to forfeit unvested equity. These last results suggest that private equity firms implement greater pay-for-performance than public company investors. If this is the case, it suggests one area where public company boards can do better.

11. HOW HAVE U.S. PUBLIC COMPANIES PERFORMED?

In Kaplan (2008), I argued that the U.S. economy, and particularly the U.S. corporate sector, had performed well in the previous 15 years or so, the period in which corporate governance and CEO pay have been criticized. During that period, the productivity of the U.S. economy increased substantially, both on an absolute basis and relative to other developed countries.[13] Furthermore, the U.S. stock market had performed well.

Since I wrote that article in early 2008, the U.S. economy has gone through a financial crisis and recession. The S&P 500 has declined from a peak of 1,576 in 2007 to roughly 1,350 as this is being written. At the same time, CEO pay has declined. What has happened to the operating performance of the S&P 500?

Scott Thurm of the *Wall Street Journal* recently reported that S&P 500 firms have weathered the financial crisis surprisingly well, with revenues up and debt levels down since 2007.[14] This performance is consistent with reports that U.S. companies held large amounts of cash in 2011. Figures 39 and 40 confirm those results.

Figure 39 reports earnings before interest, taxes, depreciation, and amortization (EBITDA) to sales, better known as the median operating margins; net debt (total debt net of cash) to total assets; and cash to total assets for the S&P 500 companies from 1993 to 2011. (The figure uses medians because outliers make averages difficult to interpret.)

---

[13] See Jorgenson, Ho, and Stiroh (2008) and van Ark, O'Mahoney, and Timmer (2008).

[14] Scott Thurm. "For Big Companies, Life Is Good." *Wall Street Journal*. April 8, 2012.

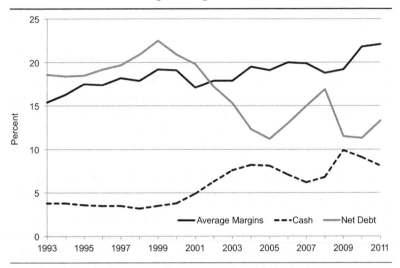

Figure 39
Median S&P 500 Operating Performance, 1993–2011

Source: COMPUSTAT.

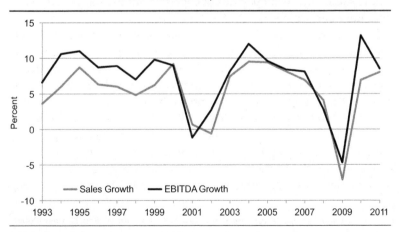

Figure 40
Median Sales and EBITDA Growth for
S&P 500 Firms, 1993–2011

Source: COMPUSTAT.

Median margins increased from 1993 to 2007. They increased again, to their highest level in the period, from 2007 to 2011. Net debt declined from 1993 to 2005, increased from 2005 to 2008, and has declined to 2006 levels in 2011. Cash holdings have generally increased from 1993 to 2009 and declined slightly since then. Figure 39 shows a picture of successful operating performance at S&P 500 companies in the first few years after 1993, and again from 2007 to 2011.

Figure 40 reports median annual sales and EBITDA growth for S&P 500 companies from 1993 to 2011. Except in 2001 and 2009, EBITDA at the median S&P 500 company has grown. On average, median EBITDA has grown 7.3 percent per year. The median company in the S&P 500 increased its revenues by almost 9 percent in 2007 and increased its EBITDA by almost 14 percent from 2007 to 2011—despite the financial crisis and recession. The performance of nonfinancial companies in the S&P 500 has been even stronger.

12. SUMMARY AND IMPLICATIONS

This paper considers the evidence for three common perceptions or criticisms of U.S. CEO pay and corporate governance: (1) CEOs are overpaid and their pay keeps increasing; (2) CEOs are not paid for performance; and (3) boards do not penalize CEOs for poor performance. The evidence is somewhat different from the perceptions.

While average CEO pay increased substantially through the 1990s, it has declined since then. CEO pay levels relative to other highly paid groups today are comparable to or lower than their average levels in the early 1990s. The ratio of large-company CEO pay to firm market value is similar to its levels in the late 1970s and lower than its pre-1960s levels. And the pay for large-company CEOs relative to other high earners is comparable to its level in the early 1990s and modestly higher than in the late 1930s.

On average, CEOs, are paid for performance and penalized for poor performance, with a large fraction of stock options and restricted stock in the typical CEO pay package.

Finally, boards do monitor CEOs, and that monitoring appears to have increased over time. CEO tenures in the 2000s are lower than in the 1980s and 1990s. And CEO turnover is tied to poor stock performance.

Shareholders largely approve of the current state of executive pay and corporate governance. In the first year of the Dodd-Frank mandated say-on-pay votes (2011), top executive pay policies received majority shareholder support at roughly 98 percent of S&P 500 and Russell 3000 companies.

Murphy (2012) concludes his impressive and detailed survey of executive compensation with the finding that executive compensation is affected by the interaction of a competitive market for talent, managerial power, and political factors. That conclusion is hard to disagree with.

There have been corporate governance failures and pay outliers where managerial power surely was exercised. And CEO pay levels are still very high relative to the typical household or person. Those are sources of the common perceptions. That said, a meaningful part of CEO pay appears to have been driven by the market for talent. In recent decades, CEO pay is likely to have been affected by the same forces of technology and scale that have led to the general increase in incomes at the very top.

For researchers, this evidence still leaves a number of questions unanswered. In particular, it would be useful to quantify the relative contributions of the market for talent, managerial power, and other considerations. And there is certainly room for more work on understanding what incentives are appropriate under what circumstances, particularly in financial versus nonfinancial businesses.

As for corporate boards, this evidence explains why compensation and the role of boards are likely to remain challenging, if not controversial. The market for talent puts pressure on boards to reward their top people at competitive pay levels to both attract and retain them. At the same time, boards must be sensitive to the accurate perception that executive pay is high relative to median household income and to the negative publicity from pay and governance outliers. Those perceptions and the current lackluster economy create political and popular pressure to reward top people with less.

REFERENCES

Bakija, J., A. Cole, and B. Heim. 2012. "Jobs and Income Growth of Top Earners and the Causes of Changing Income Inequality: Evidence from U.S. Tax Return Data." Working paper. Indiana University.

Bebchuk, Lucian, and Jesse Fried. 2006. *Pay without Performance: The Unfulfilled Promise of Executive Compensation*. Cambridge, MA: Harvard University Press.

Bertrand, Marianne, and Sendhil Mullainathan. 2001. "Are CEOs Rewarded for Luck? The Ones Without Principals Are." *Quarterly Journal of Economics* 116 (3): 901–32.

Cronqvist, Henrik, and Rüdiger Fahlenbrach. 2011. "CEO Contract Design: How Do Strong Principals Do It?" Working paper. Swiss Finance Institute Research Paper No. 11–14.

Equilar. 2011. "An Analysis of Voting Results and Performance at Russell 3000 Companies." Available online at http://www.equilar.com/knowledge-network/research-articles/2011/201107–voting-analytics.php.

Fernandes, Nuno G., Miguel A. Ferreira, Pedro P. Matos, and Kevin J. Murphy. 2011. "Are U.S. CEOs Paid More? New International Evidence." Working paper. University of Southern California.

Frydman, Carola. 2007. "The Evolution of the Market for Corporate Executives across the Twentieth Century." *Journal of Economic History* 67 (2): 488–92.

Frydman, Carola, and Dirk Jenter. 2010. "CEO Compensation." *Annual Review of Financial Economics* 2: 75–102.

Frydman, Carola, and Raven E. Saks. 2010. "Executive Compensation: A New View from a Long-Term Perspective, 1936–2005." *Review of Financial Studies* 23 (5): 2099–138.

Gabaix, Xavier, and Augustin Landier. 2008. "Why Has CEO Pay Increased So Much?" *Quarterly Journal of Economics* 123 (1): 49–100.

Hall, Brian, and Jeffrey Liebman. 1998. "Are CEOs Really Paid Like Bureaucrats?" *Quarterly Journal of Economics* 113 (3): 653–91.

Hewitt, Gary, and Carol Bowie. 2011. "Evaluating Pay for Performance Alignment: ISS' Quantitative and Qualitative Approach." White paper. Institutional Shareholder Services.

Holmstrom, Bengt, and Steven Kaplan. 2001. "Corporate Governance and Merger Activity in the United States: Making Sense of the 1980s and 1990s." *Journal of Economic Perspectives* 15 (2): 121–44.

Jenter, Dirk, and Katharina Lewellen. 2010. "Performance-Induced CEO Turnover." Working paper. Stanford University.

Jorgenson, Dale, Mun Ho, and Kevin Stiroh. 2008. "A Retrospective Look at the U.S. Productivity Growth Resurgence." *Journal of Economic Perspectives* 22 (1): 3–24.

Kaplan, Steven. 2008. "Are U.S. CEOs Overpaid?" *Academy of Management Perspectives* 22 (2): 5–16.

Kaplan, Steven, and Bernadette Minton. 2012. "How Has CEO Turnover Changed?" *International Review of Finance* 12: 57–87.

Kaplan, Steven, and Joshua Rauh. 2010. "Wall Street and Main Street: What Contributes to the Rise in the Highest Incomes?" *Review of Financial Studies* 23 (3): 1004–50.

Kroll, Luisa K., and Kerry A. Dolan. "The Forbes 400: The Richest People in America, 2011." *Forbes*, September 21, 2011.

Metrick, Andrew, and Ayako Yasuda. 2010. "The Economics of Private Equity Funds." *Review of Financial Studies* 23 (6): 2303–41.

Mishra, Subodh. 2012. "Parsing the Vote: CEO Pay Characteristics Relative to Shareholder Dissent." Working paper. Institutional Shareholder Services.

Murphy, Kevin J. 2011. "The Politics of Pay: A Legislative History of Executive Compensation." Working paper. University of Southern California.

———. Forthcoming. "Executive Compensation: Where We Are, and How We Got There." In *Handbook of the Economics of Finance*, eds. George Constantinides, Milton Harris, and René Stulz. Amsterdam: North-Holland.

——— and Ján Zábojník. 2008. "Managerial Capital and the Market for CEOs." Queen's University Economics Department Working Paper 1110.

Parker, Jonathan A., and Annette Vissing-Jørgensen. 2010. "The Increase in Income Cyclicality of High-Income Households and Its Relation to the Rise in Top Income Shares." *Brookings Papers on Economic Activity* 41 (2): 1–70.

149

Peters, Florian, and Alexander Wagner. 2012. "The Executive Turnover Risk Premium." Working paper. Swiss Finance Institute Research Paper No. 08–11.

Philippon, Thomas, and Ariell Reshef. 2008. "Wages and Human Capital in the U.S. Financial Industry: 1909–2006." Working paper. New York University.

Piketty, Thomas, and Emmanuel Saez. 2003. "Income Inequality in the United States, 1913–1998." *Quarterly Journal of Economics* 118 (1): 1–39.

———. 2006. "The Evolution of Top Incomes: A Historical and International Perspective." *American Economic Review* 96 (2): 200–206.

Taylor, Lucian A. 2010. "Why Are CEOs Rarely Fired? Evidence from Structural Estimation." *Journal of Finance* 65 (6): 2051–87.

Thomas, Randall, Alan Palmiter, and James Cotter. 2011. "Frank-Dodd's Say on Pay: Will It Lead to a Greater Role for Shareholders in Corporate Governance?" Working paper. Vanderbilt University Law and Economics Research Paper No. 11–49.

Van Ark, Bart, Mary O'Mahoney, and Marcel Timmer. 2008. "The Productivity Gap between Europe and the United States: Trends and Causes." *Journal of Economic Perspectives* 22 (1): 25–44.

Comment

Carola Frydman

The rapid rise in the level of executive compensation and the transformation in the structure of pay contracts in American publicly traded corporations since the 1980s has sparked a lively but as yet unresolved academic debate on the sources of those changes. While many different theories have been proposed, two main views—the managerial power theory and the efficient contracting theory—are predominant. Succinctly, the managerial power view argues that executive pay is the result of rent extraction by chief executive officers that control corporate boards. Pay levels are, therefore, inefficient. In contrast, defenders of the efficient contracting theory state that the competitive labor market for managerial talent determines pay, and that corporate boards attempt to align the incentives of CEOs to those of shareholders.

In his paper, Steven Kaplan presents a wide array of stylized facts to dispel some of the commonly held perceptions on executive compensation. Undeniable cases of failure in corporate governance and egregious high levels of pay give credence to the managerial power view. But while the pay of some executives likely results from rent extraction, establishing whether or not this mechanism determines the compensation of the typical CEO is not easily done. The author argues that aggregate data on executive compensation and turnover, at least for the representative CEO, are more consistent with the efficient contracting view.

Many of the stylized facts won't be surprising to researchers familiar with the executive compensation literature and with Kaplan's previous work. His important contribution in this paper is bringing together an extremely large set of facts and offering a

Carola Frydman is an assistant professor of economics at Boston University and a faculty research fellow of the National Bureau of Economic Research.

cohesive interpretation of them. Overall, I agree with the basic premises. These are the main facts we have to contend with if we hope to establish why executive compensation has evolved in a particular way. The interpretation of the facts is more difficult, and I suggest a few areas in which further study is required to strengthen our understanding of the evidence. I argue that a dichotomous debate between rent extraction and efficient contracting has been somewhat stifling for academic research, with each camp providing a rationalization for each characteristic of real compensation contracts (Frydman and Jenter 2011). As Kevin J. Murphy (forthcoming) convincingly argues, advancing our knowledge will require addressing the numerous complexities of executive pay.

PERCEPTIONS, FACTS, AND INTERPRETATION

Kaplan contends with two main perceptions regarding the *level* of executive pay. First, the increase in the real level of total pay was only marked during the 1990s, particularly for CEOs of S&P 500 firms. Over the last decade, executive compensation has declined for the average executive and remained roughly constant for the median CEO. This fact, it is argued, dispels the commonly held view that executive pay has steadily increased in recent decades.

Kaplan focuses less on the different patterns of the median and the mean, yet this difference is actually quite informative. Because the distribution of compensation is highly skewed, the mean tends to be influenced by outliers whereas the median is a better measure of compensation for the typical executive. Thus, the decline in average pay suggests that extremely large paychecks have not been as common during the last decade as they were in the 1990s. A defender of the managerial power hypothesis could therefore argue that rent extraction was a significant force behind the rise in pay during the 1990s, and that those "excessive" levels of pay have started to correct themselves in the 21st century.

The second and, I believe, more relevant perception regarding the level of pay is that CEOs are overpaid. Pay levels are undeniably high but, as Kaplan correctly emphasizes, the real question is whether these high levels are excessive or optimal. The author presents a series of facts to argue that the latter view is the more plausible interpretation. First, adjusting total CEO pay for the likelihood of losing the executive job would probably indicate lower executive pay over the past two decades since job separations have become more common. Moreover, the pay of a typical CEO has been constant relative to the market value of firms. Finally, several other occupations—such as executives of privately held firms, hedge fund managers, lawyers, and sports stars—have experienced equally rapid increases in remuneration. This fact is relevant for two reasons. Some of these jobs may be valid outside options for executives of publicly held firms. If compensation increases in the financial sector, for example, other companies will have to raise their remuneration of CEOs to retain executive talent. Moreover, these companies suffer less from the corporate governance problems that affect publicly traded firms, such as lack of observability of the manager's productivity. Since the rise in pay over time for these occupations cannot be explained by a rent extraction motive, the paper suggests that this theory is unlikely to explain the similar increase in the remuneration of CEOs of publicly traded firms.

In my view, Kaplan's argument highlights how difficult it is to determine the relevant labor market for top executives and what constitutes valid outside options for talented executives. Remuneration for managerial jobs in privately held firms seems a more appropriate comparison than the earnings of sports stars or, to some extent, lawyers. Moreover, precisely because the governance of publicly traded firms is prone to monitoring and information problems not present in other types of organizations, it is possible that the factors driving compensation patterns differ, to some substantial degree, across occupations.

A better understanding of these issues is necessary if we hope to determine what the optimal level of pay is in practice. A competitive labor market model would set remuneration to compensate for the value of the marginal product of labor. In bargaining or principal–agent models, the level of pay would, to some extent, depend on the best outside option. Some have argued that CEO candidates are able to extract large rents during the hiring process (Khurana 2002); others view a competitive labor market as a better description of the matching process between CEOs and firms (Gabaix and Landier 2008). The competitive model faces a further challenge because firms competing for talent would need to bid up the level of pay if some firms offered higher wages to attract talent, leading to widespread overpayment (Acharya and Volpin 2010).

153

Regarding the *structure* of contracts, Kaplan's paper dispels two related perceptions. While some believe that executive pay is not linked to firm performance, a comparison of firms of similar size reveals that executive pay is higher following years of good performance. A second perception is that boards do not punish CEOs for poor performance. However, the likelihood of separation, which has increased in recent decades, is higher following poor performance, particularly when boards are independent. These are important facts, deserving of attention. As difficult as it is to set the structure of pay optimally, contracts appear to be moving in the right direction as boards increasingly reward CEOs for good performance and punish them for bad outcomes.[1]

LEARNING FROM THE LONG-RUN TRENDS IN PAY

The compensation of top executives has been a contentious issue, and the discussion has remained remarkably consistent since the separation of corporate ownership from corporate control at the turn of the 20th century. During the Roaring Twenties, the U.S. government started to investigate the pay of executives in high-compensation industries like finance and transportation. Defenders of the managerial ranks argued,

> Some of our railroad men get big salaries. What of it? They earn them. . . . All these men, and thousands more in many fields of service, see clearly, think accurately, trust their judgment, and take the risk. . . . Executives are rare, so rare that they get big salaries—and smaller men snarl at them. But progress depends on such exceptional men, and we should trust them with our biggest tasks and concede them the rewards that genius and grit deserve.[2]

Fortunately, and unique to the American experience, we do not need to rely on public opinion about the size of executive pay in earlier decades because we have quantitative information. Following

---

[1] It is important to note that increasing the correlation of pay to firm performance is not always an improvement. For example, compensation contracts may give CEOs an incentive to take on too much risk. An interesting area for future research would be to better assess the distortions introduced by the structure of contracts.

[2] Boston News Bureau. "They Earn Their Salaries" (editorial). *Wall Street Journal.* February 27, 1923.

the Great Depression, the newly established Securities and Exchange Commission began requiring the disclosure of executive pay for all publicly traded corporations. Thus, compensation can be tracked fairly consistently since the 1930s. The long-run changes in compensation and in the market for managers are revealing. First, the median level of pay was much lower from the 1940s to the 1970s, a period in which the governance of firms was arguably much weaker than it has been in the recent decades. Moreover, sharp changes occurred in the late 1970s: the level of pay increased at rates that had not been seen before; the use of equity-based pay became an increasingly large fraction of compensation packages; executives began moving across corporations and even across industries late in their careers, and total pay, which had until then been unrelated to the aggregate growth of firms, became highly correlated with the size of the typical publicly traded corporation (see, for example, Frydman 2007, Murphy and Zábojník 2008, Frydman and Saks 2010).

Theories that attempt to explain the changes in executive pay in recent decades will have to confront the evolution of the long-run trends as well. For example, it is possible that the increase in firm scale, coupled with competition for managerial talent, accounts for the growth in pay since the 1980s. But was talent any less scarce during the 1950s and 1960s, when the size of firms expanded at a similar pace? If not, what other market-based or institutional differences can explain the differential paths in pay and managerial careers between these two periods?

IT'S COMPLICATED AND CHALLENGING

To most individuals knowledgeable about the long-run trends in income inequality in the United States, the evolution of executive compensation over time may not seem so surprising. CEO pay remained low when the distribution of income was compressed, and it grew as the society became more unequal. To account for the changes in income inequality over the 20th century, researchers have mostly focused on the interactions among skill-biased technological change, the relative supply and demand for skills, and various institutions that affect the distribution of earnings (see, e.g., Goldin and Katz 2010). The factors that explain the evolution of income inequality are complex and intertwined, and this insight seems also applicable to executive compensation. In a forthcoming article, Murphy argues that any convincing explanation of executive compensation would be intrinsically complicated. Kaplan's paper echoes this view, and I concur. I am hopeful that future research will be inspired by the work on income inequality and will attempt to link, both theoretically and empirically, the interactions among scale effects, the relative supply of and demand for managerial talent, corporate governance, and the various regulations that affect how firms remunerate their executives.

An assessment of these complexities is relevant for two main reasons. First, a better understanding of the determinants of compensation would be central for public policy. Given that regulations may have unexpected or undesirable consequences, future policies should be grounded in a detailed understanding of managerial markets. Second, structuring the academic debate around two opposing views—managerial power versus efficient contracting—has been somewhat counterproductive for academic research. In a recent literature review, Dirk Jenter and I found that most characteristics of real world compensation contracts have been interpreted as consistent with *either* view (Frydman and Jenter 2010). Based on such cross-sectional evidence, siding with either camp is problematic. Thus, one challenge for future theoretical work is to produce testable predictions that can differentiate between the two approaches.

Although the debate is often cast as opposing views, these two hypotheses are not mutually exclusive. Better theoretical and empirical understanding of the interactions between efficient contracting and managerial power—as well as the regulations that affect managerial contracts—may greatly further our knowledge. Another remaining challenge is to generate a more detailed knowledge of how the labor market for executives works. Learning more about hiring and promotion decisions and executives' career paths and choices may help better guide our models in the future.

REFERENCES

Acharya, Viral V., and Paolo F. Volpin. 2010. "Corporate Governance Externalities." *Review of Finance* 14 (1): 1–33.

Frydman, Carola. 2007. "Rising through the Ranks: The Evolution of the Market for Corporate Executives, 1936–2003." Working paper. Harvard University.

Frydman, Carola, and Dirk Jenter. 2010. "CEO Compensation." *Annual Review of Financial Economics* 2: 75–102.

Frydman, Carola, and Raven E. Saks. 2010. "Executive Compensation: A New View from a Long-Term Perspective, 1936–2005." *Review of Financial Studies* 23 (5): 2099–138.

Gabaix, Xavier, and Augustin Landier. 2008. "Why Has CEO Pay Increased So Much?" *Quarterly Journal of Economics* 123 (1): 49–100.

Goldin, Claudia, and Lawrence F. Katz. 2010. *The Race between Education and Technology*. Cambridge, MA: Harvard University Press.

Khurana, Rakesh. 2002. *Searching for a Corporate Savior: The Irrational Quest for Charismatic CEOs*. Princeton, NJ: Princeton University Press.

Murphy, Kevin J. Forthcoming. "Executive Compensation: Where We Are, and How We Got There." In *Handbook of the Economics of Finance*, eds. George Constantinides, Milton Harris, and René Stulz. Amsterdam: North-Holland.

Murphy, Kevin J., and Jan Zábojník. 2008. "Managerial Capital and the Market for CEOs." Queen's Economics Department Working Paper 1110.

Comment

Lucian Taylor

I believe the facts Steven Kaplan presents, and I also mainly believe his interpretation. Although some of these views may be controversial among the general public, neither the facts nor the interpretation will come as a surprise to researchers working in this area. As Kaplan points out, the paper mainly surveys existing research. However, his paper performs an important service by communicating some recent research on these topics to the public.

Kaplan's paper just scratches the surface of a very large body of research on executive pay and governance. The first part of my comment provides a few more facts about pay and governance from other research papers. The second part of my discussion argues that facts are not enough, and that we sometimes need theory to help us interpret the facts.

BLOCKHOLDERS

Corporate governance aims to solve agency problems. Shareholders are the principal, and the chief executive officer and other top executives are the agents. The question here is how we can make sure a firm is being run in shareholders' best interests, given that the shareholders cannot run the firm themselves. Shareholders must hire CEOs and other top executives to run the firm, but those executives' interests may not align with shareholders' interests.

There are two main ways we get executives to do the right thing for shareholders in two ways. First, we provide them with incentives: we tie their pay to the firm's performance, and we threaten to fire them if the firm performs poorly. Second, we monitor them. Shareholders hire the corporate board of directors to monitor the CEO.

Lucian "Luke" Taylor is an assistant professor of finance in the Wharton School of the University of Pennsylvania.

For example, the CEO will likely need the board's approval before acquiring another company. It also falls on the board to provide the CEO with the right incentives—that is, to set the CEO's compensation contract and potentially replace the CEO.

But who makes sure the board is acting in shareholders' best interests? Directors are themselves agents whose interests are not necessarily aligned with shareholders' interests. In other words, there is a second layer of principal–agent conflict between shareholders and the board. In theory, we can solve this second agency like we solved the first one, through providing incentives and direct monitoring. We give boards several types of incentives: directors typically own shares in the firm, so their wealth is tied to the firm's performance; shareholders can replace directors after bad performance; and directors care about their reputation.

Moving up one level, who monitors the board, and who makes sure the board has the right incentives? This is a crucial question, because if boards are not acting in shareholders' interests, there is little hope that the CEO will act in shareholders' interests. As the picture suggests, it is shareholders who need to monitor the board and make sure the board has the right incentives. But the problem is this: if the typical shareholder is small, then what incentives do shareholders have to make sure the board is doing its job? If you are anything like me, your investments are diversified across many companies. Your ownership of any single company is so small that you do not have much incentive to make sure that company's board is doing its job. A firm's many small shareholders would have difficulty coordinating with each other.

One potential solution is government intervention. We could create laws that ensure the board has strong enough incentives and let regulators monitor the board. That way, shareholders would know they are buying a "safe" product when they invest in a company, just like we know we are buying a safe drug when we go to the pharmacy, thanks to the Food and Drug Administration's oversight.

The good news is that we do not need government intervention to solve this problem, because there is a market solution. The solution to this problem is to let a large shareholder, called a blockholder, monitor the board. The blockholder's large stake in the company provides an incentive to figure out whether the board is doing its job and to intervene if it is not. Thus, blockholders can make this governance system work well.

Blockholders are pervasive. Here are some facts from a recent paper by Holderness (2009):

- Some 96 percent of U.S. public firms have a blockholder, defined as a shareholder who owns at least 5 percent of the shares.
- Blockholders own 39 percent of a firm, on average.
- Three times as many firms have a majority blockholder as have no blockholder.
- Ownership is less concentrated in larger firms, but even 89 percent of S&P 500 firms have blockholders.
- Ownership concentration in the United States is similar to concentration in other countries.

Since blockholders are pervasive and have a strong incentive to monitor boards of directors, we have some hope that boards are acting in shareholders' interests.

WHAT HAPPENS TO CEOS WHO GET FIRED?

Citing research by Jenter and Lewellen (2010), Kaplan shows that poorly performing CEOs are much more likely to leave their firm. Presumably, many of those CEOs were fired. An important follow-on question is whether being fired is costly to a CEO. If not, then the threat of being fired does not provide CEOs with a strong incentive to perform.

CEOs typically receive separation pay upon leaving the firm, which makes being fired less costly to the CEO. Goldman and Huang (2010) collect data on separation payouts to 609 S&P 500 CEOs who left office between 1993 and 2007. Only 287 of those CEOs received a separation payout, so the median separation payout was zero. For those CEOs who received a nonzero payout, the average payout was $9.5 million, which is roughly 290 percent of their average annual salary. The $9.5 million amount pools together CEOs who leave the firm voluntarily and those who are fired. From Yermack (2006), we know that separation pay is several times higher if the CEO was forced out of the firm. To the extent that CEOs expect a separation payout upon being fired, the payouts soften the blow and make the threat of dismissal a weaker incentive for CEOs.

One cost of being fired is that it is potentially harder to find a new job. Fee and Hadlock (2004) examine the future employment outcomes for S&P 500 CEOs who left their jobs between 1993 and 1998. They show that for executives under age 60 who were forced out, only 34 percent found future work in an executive role ($n = 253$). For executives under age 60 who left as part of a scandal, only 13 percent found future work in an executive role ($n = 16$). For CEOs who left the firm and did manage to become CEO elsewhere, the median new firm was 90 percent smaller ($n = 12$). Since executive pay is strongly positively correlated with firm size, this last result suggests that those CEOs took a large pay cut. These results together suggest that executives do have trouble finding high-quality jobs after they are forced out of the firm, which provides CEOs with an incentive to perform well and avoid being fired.

COMPENSATION PEER GROUPS

As Kaplan points out, there are examples of "corporate governance failures and pay outliers where managerial power surely was exercised." He argues that the problems are mainly outliers and isolated cases. However, examples of "managerial power" are widespread and easily found, not just a case of a few outliers. Next I provide one example.

When setting a CEO's pay, the board's compensation committee typically benchmarks the pay level against the pay level in a peer group of similar firms. The choice of peer group is subjective and at the firm's discretion. For example, in 2006 the pharmaceutical firm Pfizer stated, "The Committee sets midpoint salaries, target bonus levels, and target annual long-term incentive award values at the median of a peer group of pharmaceutical companies and a general industry comparator group of Fortune 100 companies." (Faulkender and Yang 2010). The pharmaceutical peers included Abbott Labs, Amgen, Merck, and a few other firms. The "general industry comparator group" included several firms that look quite different from Pfizer, including Walt Disney, Wells Fargo, General Motors, and others.

The potential problem is that CEOs may wield power over their pay by convincing the compensation committee to choose a favorable set of peer firms. In other words, firms may be able to cherry pick the peer group so as to pay the CEO as much as they want.

In 2006, the Securities and Exchange Commission required that firms start disclosing which other firms they choose as their peer group. Faulkender and Yang (2010) analyzed data on firms' choice of peer group. They found that firms tend to choose highly paid peers to justify their high CEO compensation. In other words, firms do appear to cherry pick peer firms with high pay. The effect is especially strong when the peer group is smaller, the CEO is the chairman of the board, the CEO has longer tenure, and the directors are busy serving on multiple boards. Their interpretation is that CEOs can wield power over the level of pay via the choice of peer group, especially in firms with weaker governance. This manifestation of managerial power is widespread across firms, not a matter of a few outliers.

FACTS ARE GREAT, BUT MODELS HELP, TOO

Kaplan's paper presents many empirical facts, which provides a great service. However, next I will try to argue that facts alone are not enough. Models sometimes provide surprising, counterintuitive lessons about what good governance looks like. Also, a model sometimes helps when interpreting the empirical facts. The following example, drawn from Taylor (2010), illustrates this point.

According to data from 1970 to 2006, on average roughly 2 percent of CEOs are fired per year. (The rate has gone up in recent years, a point I will come back to.) Total CEO turnover is higher than 2 percent per year, but most turnovers represent voluntary successions rather than firings. The 2 percent firing rate seems low, and it is tempting to conclude that CEOs are entrenched and directors are not acting in shareholders' interests.

However, the literature provides little guidance for making such judgments. For example, it is not clear what firing rate we should expect from a well-functioning board. Therefore, it is difficult to judge whether the observed 2 percent rate is low or high. If it is indeed too low, it is not clear how much shareholder value is being destroyed.

My goal (in Taylor 2010) was to provide a benchmark for the CEO firing rate and to quantify the amount of shareholder value at stake. The benchmark is a model in which a rational board of directors has to decide each year whether to replace its CEO. Some CEOs have high ability, others have low ability. The board faces a tradeoff: firing a low-ability CEO will increase the firm's future profits, but in the short term, firing the CEO is costly. One complication is that we cannot directly observe a CEO's ability. Instead, we learn about it gradually over time.

By taking that model to the data, I found some interesting results:

- The 2 percent observed firing rate is indeed low, in the sense that to produce a 2 percent firing rate, boards must behave as if firing the CEO costs at least $200 million.

- There is evidence of entrenchment: Boards behave as if firing the CEO costs at least $200 million, but really it costs the firm much less to replace the CEO. The gap between the *perceived* and *actual* turnover cost indicates that boards find it very unpleasant to fire their CEO. In other words, CEOs are entrenched.

- The degree of entrenchment was 73 percent lower in 1990–2006 compared to 1971–1989, mainly because the rate of forced turnover was much higher (3 percent per year) in the later subsample.

- Using results from the 1990–2006 subsample, shareholder value would rise by just 1.4 percent if we could somehow eliminate entrenchment, all else being equal.

One question I was not able to answer (in Taylor 2010) is how much CEO entrenchment is optimal for shareholders. Zero entrenchment is probably not optimal, since firms might have a hard time attracting talented CEOs if those CEOs face a high chance of being fired.

REFERENCES

Faulkender, Michael, and Jun Yang. 2010. "Inside the Black Box: The Role and Composition of Compensation Peer Groups." *Journal of Financial Economics* 96 (2): 257–70.

Fee, C. Edward, and Charles J. Hadlock. 2004. "Management Turnover across the Corporate Hierarchy." *Journal of Accounting and Economics* 37: 3–38.

Goldman, Eitan, and Peggy Huang. 2010. "Contractual versus Actual Pay following CEO Departure." Working paper. Indiana University.

Holderness, Clifford. 2009. "The Myth of Diffuse Ownership in the United States." *Review of Financial Studies* 22 (4): 1377–1408.

Jenter, Dirk, and Katharina Lewellen. 2010. "Performance-Induced CEO Turnover." Working paper. Stanford University.

Taylor, Lucian A. 2010. "Why Are CEOs Rarely Fired? Evidence from Structural Estimation." *Journal of Finance* 65 (6): 2051–87.

Yermack, David. 2006. "Golden Handshakes: Separation Pay for Retired and Dismissed CEOs." *Journal of Accounting and Economics* 41 (3): 237–56.

General Equilibrium Effects of Prison on Crime: Evidence from International Comparisons

Justin McCrary and Sarath Sanga

ABSTRACT

We compare crime and incarceration rates over time for the United States, Canada, and England and Wales, as well as for a small selection of comparison countries. Shifts in U.S. punishment policy led to a five-fold increase in the incarceration rate, while nearly every other country experienced only minor increases in incarceration. The large shifts in U.S. punishment policy do not seem to have caused commensurately large improvements in public safety.

Justin McCrary is a professor of law in the School of Law at the University of California, Berkeley and a faculty research fellow of the National Bureau of Economic Research.

Sarath Sanga is a law student at Yale Law School.

General Equilibrium Effects of Prison on Crime: Evidence from International Comparisons

1. INTRODUCTION

From 1920 through 1970, the rate of incarceration in the United States was roughly constant, hovering around 100 per 100,000. Today, the incarceration rate is five times that level. The incarceration rate in the United States is thus markedly higher today than it was historically.

The incarceration rate in the United States is also markedly higher today than it is in other countries. According to the International Centre for Prison Studies of the University of Essex, in 2008 the United States accounted for 5 percent of world population but 23 percent of worldwide prisoners (Walmsley 2009).

Figure 1 displays the time series of the incarceration rate for the United States as compared with that of other countries. Panel A compares the United States to Canada and England and Wales (combined) over the last century. These countries have perhaps the longest tradition of collecting data on incarceration rates and are additionally relatively comparable to one another in terms of language, economy, law, and culture. The figure indicates that already during the early part of the 20th century, the United States had higher incarceration rates than Canada and England and Wales. From 1925 through 1970, however, those countries essentially caught up to the United States. But starting in 1970, the United States made substantial investments in prison capacity, and by 2010 the U.S. incarceration rate was 3.3 times that of England and Wales and 4.4 times that of Canada. These conclusions are particularly stark; compared to other countries that are members of the Organization for Economic Cooperation and Development, England and Wales have a relatively high incarceration rate.

Panel B compares the United States to selected OECD countries over the last four decades.[1] The figure indicates that the U.S. increase

---

[1] Throughout this paper, countries were selected on grounds of data availability and quality.

Figure 1
Incarceration Rates in Perspective

A. *U.S., England & Wales, and Canada: 1870 to present*

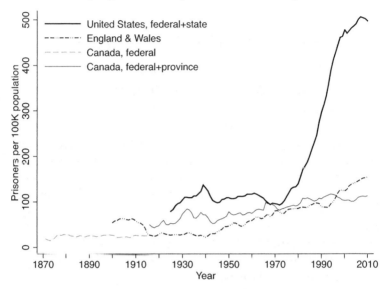

B. *Selected Rich Countries: 1970 to present*

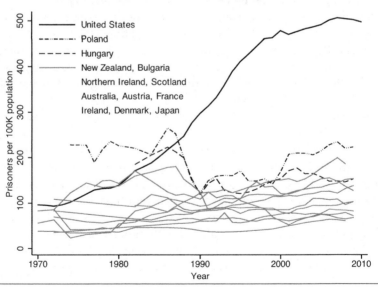

Source: See text, pp. 170–71, 173.

168

in incarceration is surprising compared to Canada and England and Wales, as well as to a broader set of countries.

In sum, from a historical and comparative perspective, the expanded use of prisons in the United States in recent decades is breathtaking. However, while the punitiveness of the current U.S. system is unusual, some people may be willing to set aside the obvious liberty concerns if they are persuaded that prison is sufficiently effective at providing for the safety of those not imprisoned. Scholars and policymakers alike note that a large prison system could reduce crime through two important channels: deterrence and incapacitation. Assessing the magnitude of these channels is an important task for research and one that is taken up in an extensive academic literature.

However, a general equilibrium policy evaluation of the increased use of imprisonment must take account of additional possible mechanisms. One such mechanism is the so-called prison reentry problem, which has been much discussed in the popular press recently and in the academic literature. Nationally, roughly 700,000 people will be released from prison (long-term incarceration) this year, and roughly 7 million people will be released from jail (short-term incarceration). It is conceivable that those released will be changed by virtue of the experience of incarceration. Such changes could be protective against crime if, for example, former prisoners decided to "go straight" to avoid any subsequent confinement. More concerning is the possibility that the changes could encourage crime if, for example, former prisoners found themselves unable to obtain legitimate work and were thereby encouraged to engage in crime, or if they were scarred by the experience and unable to cope with life on the outside.

A second such mechanism is the replacement hypothesis (Freeman 1999). In Freeman's view, criminal opportunities are limited and rivalrous—if one person is taking advantage of the opportunity, another cannot take advantage of it simultaneously—and the group of potential offenders is large relative to the number of criminal opportunities. Accordingly, if this mechanism is important, incapacitation could be entirely offset by replacement. In simple terms, one corner drug dealer is sent to prison, and another steps forward to take his place.

A third mechanism is the effect of the scope of imprisonment on deterrence via externality. Typically, deterrence is framed as an individual's decreased inclination toward crime because of a higher threatened sanction. However, the stigma associated with a criminal record may be an important deterrent as well, for example in the labor market or in social interactions. Stigma means that in the extreme, higher threatened sanctions can be counterproductive (Rasmusen 1996). In simple terms, when punishment is rare, a punished person is more likely to be a bad seed than when punishment is prevalent.

The research designs used in the literature focus on measurement of deterrence and incapacitation and are unable to capture these broader general equilibrium phenomena. In the literature, general equilibrium policy evaluation has primarily been done in the context of formal structural modeling of the potential offenders' economic and legal environment (see, for example, Burdett, Lagos, and Wright 2004). This approach has many merits, including the clear explication of mechanisms and a natural methodology for evaluating counterfactual policy experiments.

In this paper, we complement the theoretical literature with an empirical assessment of the general equilibrium effects of mass incarceration. Our approach is rooted in the observation that the magnitude of the expansion in the prison population in the United States over the last 40 years has been nearly unique internationally. Our conclusions are informed by a new data set on the use of imprisonment and the extent of crime for a large group of countries over many years. We pay particularly close attention to Canada and to England and Wales, as these are natural comparisons for the United States, and the governments of those countries have a tradition of collecting the relevant data.

The plan for the paper is as follows: Section 2 describes the data we use. Section 3 focuses on a comparative analysis of trends in the United States, Canada, and England and Wales. Section 4 introduces some simple panel data regressions to summarize the results. Section 5 concludes.

2. DATA

Our first analysis compares the United States to Canada. Data on crime in Canada are taken from the *Statistics Canada* website, www.statcan.gc.ca. Data on prisoners in Canada are taken from the *Statistics Canada* website for 1978 to the present. Historical data on prisoners were obtained from Tables Z173–174 (federal prisoners) and Tables Z198–208 (provincial prisoners) of *Historical Statistics of Canada* (2nd edition). Data on U.S. crime are taken from the Federal

Bureau of Investigation's *Uniform Crime Reports*. Data on U.S. prisoners are taken from the University at Albany's *Sourcebook of Criminal Justice Statistics*.

Our second analysis compares the United States to England and Wales. Data on crime for the latter are taken from two electronic files produced by the Home Office, "Recorded Crime Statistics 1898–2001/2" and "Recorded Crime Statistics 2002/3–2009/10." Data on prisoners are taken from Table 7.5 of "Offender Management Caseload Statistics 2009."

Our final analysis uses data from the *Surveys of Crime Trends and Operations of Criminal Justice Systems*. These data were collected by the Crime Prevention and Criminal Justice Division of the United Nations ("UN data") in 10 separate waves. The data collection for the first wave was conducted in 1978 and pertained to aspects of crime and the criminal justice system for the years 1970–75. Subsequent waves were collected roughly every five years; the most recent information from the survey pertains to 2006. All of the statistics reported in the survey are collected from statistical reports from the respondent countries. We have hand-checked these data using Eurostat data, which are available after 1987. We have observed some minor discrepancies between the values in the survey and those in the Eurostat data, but these seem to emerge from definitional differences.

Perhaps oddly, a counterexample is the UN data set for the United States. Fortunately, high-quality data for the United States are available from several other sources, and we have replaced the U.S. values in the UN data with information from the *Sourcebook*. For other countries, our sense is that the main measurement problem in the survey emerges from nonresponse rather than incorrect values.

3. COMPARISON WITH CANADA AND ENGLAND AND WALES

Previous research has noted that, despite substantial similarity between the two countries on many dimensions, Canada does not imprison its citizens at nearly the rate the United States does (Doob and Webster 2006). Figure 2A displays total incarceration rates per 100,000 using publicly available data for Canada and the United States. The figure indicates that Canada did not increase its use of prisons over the

Figure 2
Imprisonment and Crime: United States and Canada

A. *Incarceration Rate*

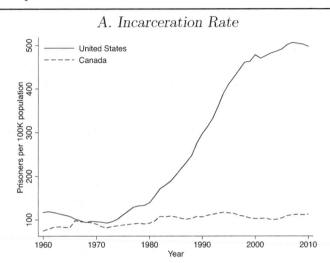

B. *Homicide Rate*

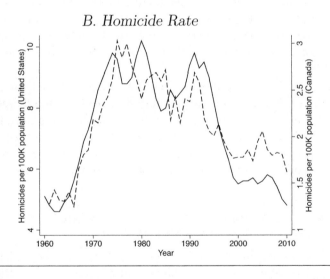

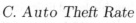

Figure 2
(continued)

C. Auto Theft Rate

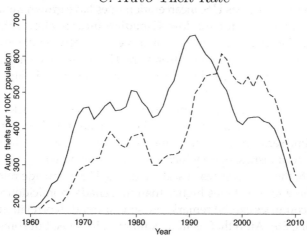

D. Robbery Rate

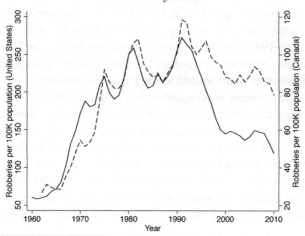

Source: See text, pp. 170–71, 174.

last 30 years in the same way that the United States did. While *Statistics Canada* presently provides a series going back only to 1978, data are available going back to 1916 in *Historical Statistics of Canada*. The figure indicates that Canada has displayed little change in incarceration rates over 40 years, whereas U.S. incarceration rates have grown rapidly.

One explanation for the low Canadian incarceration rates observed in Figure 2A is a low rate of crime: a country with a low rate of crime has little need for imprisonment. However, this is not a good explanation for the stark differences in trend observed in Figure 2A because Canadian and U.S. crime rates exhibit rather similar trends. Panels B, C, and D provide time series for the rates of homicide, auto theft, and robbery, respectively, in the two countries. These are the three crime series believed to be measured most accurately in aggregate police statistics, upon which both series are based.

Despite their differences in scale, with the U.S. homicide rate generally three to four times higher than in Canada, homicide rates in the two countries exhibit remarkably similar trends (correlation coefficient of 0.86). Auto theft is more similar in its level, but somewhat less similar in its trend. In Canada, the peak auto theft rate comes about five years after the peak rate in the United States. Panel D displays the robbery rate for the two countries. The similarity in the series is remarkable; the most prominent difference in the series is that the post-1990 decline in crime is more marked in the U.S. data. An important question is whether the faster decline in crime in the United States can be attributed to the prison expansion.

These comparisons are suggestive but largely anecdotal. Nonetheless, drawing a contrast between the United States and Canada clarifies two simple points. First, despite a variety of similarities between the two countries, the increased use of imprisonment in the United States saw little parallel in Canada. Second, the effect on crime of the large investment in prisons is hard to discern with the naked eye. The United States and Canada seem to have generally similar crime trends that may or may not be related to changes in punishment policy.

Before attempting to draw any more conclusions from these data, we pause to note a conceptual difficulty with inferring the effect of punishment policy on crime using natural variation in incarceration rates. Imprisonment is an equilibrium phenomenon that reflects both changes in punitiveness as well as changes in crime, and imprisonment both causes and is affected by crime. McCrary (2009) emphasizes the cohort decomposition of those in prison as a means of clarifying these points. Let Q_t denote the fraction of the population in prison, G_t the fraction of those not in prison who engage in crime, p_t the fraction of offenders arrested, and $H_t(s) \equiv P_t\,(S_t \geq s)$ the fraction of arrestees obtaining a sentence of at least s periods, where s is an integer. Since those in prison were either free last period and committed an offense for which they were sentenced to at least one period in prison, or were free two periods ago and committed an offense for which they were sentenced to at least two periods, and so on, we have

(1) $$Q_t = \Sigma_{s=1}^{\infty}(1 - Q_{t-s})\,G_{t-s}p_{t-s}P(S_{t-s} \geq s)$$

In the steady state, where G_t, p_t, and $H_t\,(\cdot)$ have been constant for sufficiently long that Q_t is constant, we have

(2) $$Q = (1 - Q)\,Gp\,\Sigma_{s=1}^{\infty}H(s)$$
$$\leftrightarrow Q = \frac{Gp\mathbb{E}[S]}{1 + Gp\mathbb{E}[S]} \leftrightarrow 1 - Q = \frac{1}{1 + Gp\mathbb{E}[S]}$$

where we make use of the fact that the sum of the survivor function is equal to the mean, or $\Sigma_{s=1}^{\infty}H\,(s) = \mathbb{E}[S]$. Some calculus shows that

(3) $$\frac{\partial\ln Q}{\partial\ln \mathbb{E}[S]} = (1 - Q)\,(1 + \varepsilon) < 1$$

where $\varepsilon = \partial\ln G/\partial\ln \mathbb{E}[S]$ is the elasticity of crime on the part of the free with respect to expected sentence lengths. This equation says that a 1 percent increase in the punishment schedule confronting offenders exerts less than a 1 percent increase in the incarceration rate. A standard empirical policy evaluation exercise would relate the growth rate in crime to the growth rate in imprisonment. That is, it would measure empirically the quantity $\Delta \ln C/\Delta \ln Q$, perhaps using a regression. Equation (3) shows that this approach will tend to exaggerate the effect of imprisonment on crime because the denominator is functionally related to the numerator. We will try to quantify this effect momentarily.

Outside of the steady state, we can use equation (1) to understand the dynamic effects on incarceration of a change in punishment policy. Figure 3 demonstrates the effect of an immediate shift and a slow shift in the distribution of sentence lengths on the incarceration rate with no, modest, and large deterrence effects of expected

Figure 3
Hypothetical Changes to Crime and Incarceration Rates
Associated with Increases in Sentence Lengths

A. Instantaneous Shift: Crime Effect

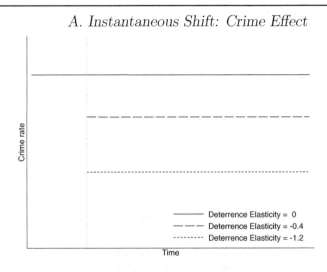

B. Gradual Shift: Crime Effect

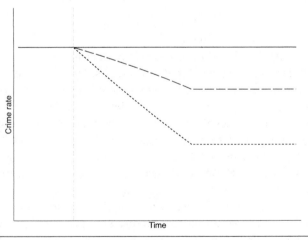

Figure 3
(continued)

C. Instantaneous Shift: Incarceration Effect

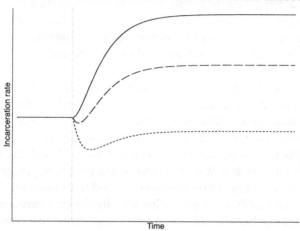

D. Gradual Shift: Incarceration Effect

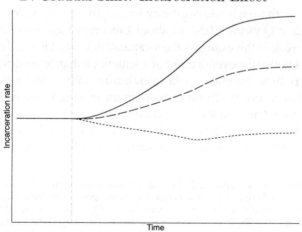

---

sentence lengths on crime.[2] Panel A shows the effect on the overall crime rate of an instantaneous and large shift to the right in the distribution of sentence lengths. The solid line shows the crime rate assuming no deterrence; the long dashed line shows the crime rate assuming a deterrence elasticity of −0.4; and the short dashed line shows the crime rate assuming a deterrence elasticity of −1.2. The solid line imperceptibly declines after the policy reform (indicated by a vertical dashed line) because of the incapacitation effect of prison. Both dashed lines show dramatic and immediate declines because of the deterrence effect.

Panel C shows the effect of this policy reform on incarceration. The solid line increases rapidly, but at a decreasing rate, converging to the new steady-state value after 300 months and to 90 percent of the steady-state value after 120 months. Prison populations evolve very slowly, like the temperature in the ocean. Empirical evidence consistent with this fact is that while crime began dropping precipitously in 1990, the U.S. prison population continued to increase for another 19 years, until 2009. The dashed line initially declines because of deterrence effects, but after 24 months the incarceration rate rises above its initial level and continues to climb to its new steady-state value. While fewer individuals cross the threshold of the prison because of deterrence, those who do must stay longer. Interestingly, computing $\Delta \ln C / \Delta \ln Q$ yields −0.67, or about 1.68 times the deterrence elasticity of −0.4. In this example, the incapacitation effect is small enough that −0.4 is also the overall effect of a sentence enhancement on crime.

Panel B shows the effect on the overall crime rate of a more plausible policy shift, which is a linear increase in the expected sentence length facing a potential offender. The solid line is essentially unchanged (the incapacitation effect is now even less perceptible), but the dashed line declines nearly linearly in time as sentence lengths increase. Panel D

[2] The example uses a geometric distribution for sentence lengths on 0, 1, 2,... so that $P(S_t \geq s) = \gamma_t^s$, where $1 - \gamma_t$ is the per-period release probability for a prisoner. We peg the steady-state values for the key variables C_t, Q_t, G_t and p_t to roughly match empirical values for the United States in recent years. The hypothetical values for G_t are then constructed using a log linear approximation to the relationship between the crime rate of the free and the mean sentence length, i.e., we adjust the crime rate as $G' = \exp(\ln G + \varepsilon \Delta \ln \mathbb{E}[S])$, where ε is the elasticity of crime with respect to the mean sentence length and $\Delta \ln \mathbb{E}[S]$ is the percent change in the mean sentence length associated with the example. Hypothetical values for Q_t are generated directly from equation (1) and the hypothetical values for C_t are generated according to the identity $C_t = (1 - Q_t)G_t$.

shows the effects of this shift on incarceration. As before, incarceration declines at first because all the prisoners are incumbents and hence the prison exit rate is unaffected, yet the prison entry rate is lower because of deterrence. The effect is hard to detect visually but lasts for about 24 months. Eventually, the exit rate from prison is reduced because enough prisoners entered after the reform in punishment policy, and incarceration climbs rapidly thereafter.

This discussion highlights the hazards of using natural variation in incarceration rates to draw inferences about the effect of prison on crime. As panel C emphasizes visually, in the short run, one sees a positive association between incarceration and crime. This follows for two reasons. First, a spike in punitiveness reduces crime faster than it increases incarceration. Second, the immediate reduction in crime that occurs reduces the flow rate into prison enough to shrink the incarceration rate, even though the long-run consequences are for higher incarceration rates. After a decade, however, we are in a long-run scenario where there is a negative association between incarceration and crime. Nonetheless, the magnitude of the association is exaggerated because of the functional relationship between incarceration and crime. Roughly speaking, the association at long-run frequencies should be discounted by roughly $1 \div 1.67$, or about 0.6. However, if the magnitude of the elasticity of crime with respect to expected sentence lengths is sufficiently large, one will observe a positive association with incarceration and crime even in the long run.

Perhaps the most important takeaway from panel C is this: holding fixed the probability of apprehension, long-run secular increases in the incarceration rate will be observed under only two conditions. First, sentence lengths have to increase. Second, the deterrence elasticity of sentence lengths cannot be too great. Were it to be substantial, the flow rate into prison would be reduced by too much for the prison population to be able to grow. Finally, note that if deterrence effects were appreciable yet inelastic, then we should observe oscillation in the prison population, with short-run prisoner-reducing effects of policy reforms on the prison population being offset by medium- and long-run prisoner-increasing effects.

Returning to the data from the United States and Canada, we now present an analysis of the long-run differences in the data. Table 1 presents growth rates in crime and incarceration rates for Canada and the United States for 1960, 1970, 1980, 1990, 2000, and 2010. Table 2

Table 1
Log Differences in Crime and Incarceration Rates

	Canada				United States			
	Murder	Auto Theft	Robbery	Prison	Murder	Auto Theft	Robbery	Prison
One decade								
1970–1960	0.9	115	28	16	2.8	274	112	−21
1980–1970	0.2	88	46	2	2.3	45	79	43
1990–1980	0.0	29	1	14	−0.8	154	6	158
2000–1990	−0.6	110	−13	−4	−3.9	−244	−112	181
2010–2000	−0.2	−250	−9	10	−0.7	−173	−26	19
Two decades								
1980–1960	1.1	203	74	18	5.1	319	191	22
1990–1970	0.2	117	47	16	1.5	199	85	201
2000–1980	−0.6	139	−12	10	−4.7	−90	−106	339
2010–1990	−0.8	−140	−23	6	−4.6	−417	−138	200
Three decades								
1990–1960	1.1	232	75	32	4.3	473	197	180
2000–1970	−0.4	227	33	12	−2.4	−45	−27	382
2010–1980	−0.8	−111	−22	20	−5.4	−263	−132	358
Four decades								
2000–1960	0.5	342	61	28	0.4	229	85	361
2010–1970	−0.6	−23	24	22	−3.1	−218	−53	401
Five decades								
2010–1960	0.3	92	52	38	−0.3	56	59	380

Table 2
Estimated Effect of Prison on Crime:
U.S.-Canadian Comparisons

	Naive			Adjusted		
	Murder	Auto Theft	Robbery	Murder	Auto Theft	Robbery
One decade						
1970–1960	−0.05	−4.32	−2.28	−0.03	−2.59	−1.37
1980–1970	0.05	−1.05	0.81	0.03	−0.63	0.49
1990–1980	−0.01	0.87	0.03	0.00	0.52	0.02
2000–1990	−0.02	−1.92	−0.53	−0.01	−1.15	−0.32
2010–2000	−0.06	8.43	−1.81	−0.04	5.06	−1.08
Two decades						
1980–1960	0.96	27.98	28.28	0.57	16.79	16.79
1990–1970	0.01	0.44	0.21	0.00	0.26	0.12
2000–1980	−0.01	−0.70	−0.29	−0.01	−0.42	−0.17
2010–1990	−0.02	−1.43	−0.59	−0.01	−0.86	−0.36
Three decades						
1990–1960	0.02	1.62	0.82	0.01	0.97	0.49
2000–1970	−0.01	−0.74	−0.16	0.00	−0.44	−0.10
2010–1980	−0.01	−0.45	−0.33	−0.01	−0.27	−0.20
Four decades						
2000–1960	0.00	−0.34	0.07	0.00	−0.20	0.04
2010–1970	−0.01	−0.52	−0.20	0.00	−0.31	−0.12
Five decades						
2010–1960	0.00	−0.11	0.02	0.00	−0.06	0.01

presents naive and adjusted estimates of the effect of punishment on crime. The naive estimates are the difference-in-difference for the given crime rate (i.e., the U.S.-Canadian difference in the temporal growth rate) relative to the difference-in-difference for the incarceration rate. The adjusted estimates are discounted by 0.6, reflecting the conceptual discussion above.

These estimates indicate that there are often quite violent swings in crime rates that have little to do with changes in penal policy. This is consistent with a potential identification problem, which is that in the medium run, changes in incarceration rates may be a response to changes in crime. Our preferred difference is the longest difference in the data. We are persuaded that the U.S.-Canadian difference in response to crime between 1960 and 2010 has less to do with crime than it has to do with politics and culture. Even if the dramatic run-up in incarceration rates in the United States were reflective of a response to crime, it was plausibly a response to the crime wave of the 1960s and 1970s, and not to current conditions.

Our preferred 2010–1960 difference indicates very small effects of prison on crime. These are consistent with zero and are generally small in magnitude. However, the 2010–1970 difference is essentially as credible on a priori grounds to us and is more consistent with the idea that prison is protective against crime. Plainly, more data are needed to triangulate.

We turn now to the data from England and Wales. Figure 4 is structured analogously to Figure 2, and Tables 3 and 4 are structured analogously to Tables 1 and 2. The results for England and Wales depend less on the base year. The estimates for both 2010–1960 and 2010–1970 indicate that prison may indeed be protective against crime.

4.   PANEL DATA REGRESSIONS

We estimate

$$(4) \qquad C_{ct} = \alpha_c + \delta_t + \gamma Q_{ct} + \epsilon_{ct}$$

where C is either robbery, homicide, or auto theft. These results are in Table 5. Table 6 lists the number of observations each country contributes to these regressions. The results are quite sensitive to specification, with the seemingly innocuous change from levels to logs changing the sign of the robbery estimate.

Figure 4
Imprisonment and Crime: United States and England and Wales

A. Incarceration Rate

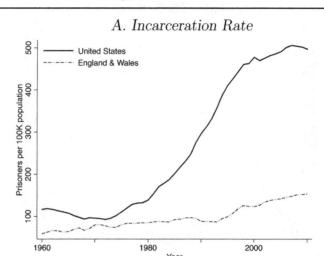

B. Homicide Rate

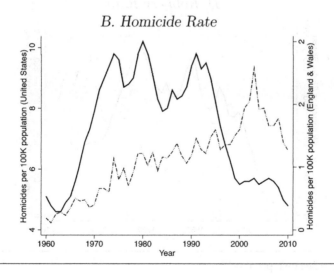

Figure 4
(continued)

C. Auto Theft Rate

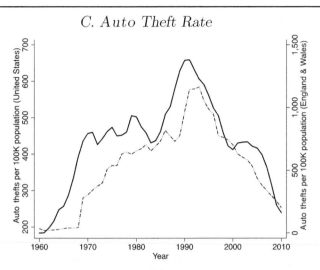

D. Robbery Rate

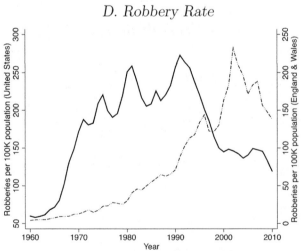

Source: See text, pp. 170–71.

Table 3
Log Differences in Crime and Incarceration Rates

	England and Wales				United States			
	Murder	Auto Theft	Robbery	Prison	Murder	Auto Theft	Robbery	Prison
One decade								
1970–1960	0.11	269.33	8.71	20.92	2.8	273.8	112.0	−21
1980–1970	0.41	350.95	17.39	5.32	2.3	45.4	79.0	43
1990–1980	−0.02	314.81	40.75	3.75	−0.8	155.6	5.9	158
2000–1990	0.21	−265.92	91.95	34.95	−3.9	−245.6	−112.0	181
2010–2000	−0.17	−502.55	−24.80	29.97	−0.7	−173.4	−25.9	19
Two decades								
1980–1960	0.52	620.28	26.09	26.24	5.1	319.2	191.0	22
1990–1970	0.39	665.76	58.13	9.07	1.5	201.0	84.9	201
2000–1980	0.19	48.89	132.70	38.70	−4.7	−90.0	−106.1	339
2010–1990	0.04	−768.47	67.15	64.92	−4.6	−419.0	−137.9	200
Three decades								
1990–1960	0.50	935.10	66.84	29.99	4.3	474.8	196.9	180
2000–1970	0.60	399.84	150.08	44.02	−2.4	−44.6	−27.1	382
2010–1980	0.02	−453.66	107.90	68.67	−5.4	−263.4	−132.0	358
Four decades								
2000–1960	0.71	669.18	158.79	64.94	0.4	229.2	84.9	361
2010–1970	0.43	−102.71	125.28	73.99	−3.1	−218.0	−53.0	401
Five decades								
2010–1960	0.54	166.63	133.99	94.91	−0.3	55.8	59.0	380

Table 4
Estimated Effect of Prison on Crime: U.S.–England and Wales Comparisons

	Naive			Adjusted		
	Murder	Auto Theft	Robbery	Murder	Auto Theft	Robbery
One decade						
1970–1960	−0.06	−0.11	−2.46	−0.04	−0.06	−1.48
1980–1970	0.05	−8.11	1.64	0.03	−4.87	0.98
1990–1980	−0.01	−1.03	−0.23	0.00	−0.62	−0.14
2000–1990	−0.03	0.14	−1.40	−0.02	0.08	−0.84
2010–2000	0.05	−30.00	0.10	0.03	−18.00	0.06
Two decades						
1980–1960	−1.08	71.02	−38.90	−0.65	42.61	−23.34
1990–1970	0.01	−2.42	0.14	0.00	−1.45	0.08
2000–1980	−0.02	−0.46	−0.80	−0.01	−0.28	−0.48
2010–1990	−0.03	2.59	−1.52	−0.02	1.55	−0.91
Three decades						
1990–1960	0.03	−3.07	0.87	0.02	−1.84	0.52
2000–1970	−0.01	−1.31	−0.52	−0.01	−0.79	−0.31
2010–1980	−0.02	0.66	−0.83	−0.01	39.00	−0.50
Four decades						
2000–1960	0.00	−1.49	−0.25	0.00	−0.89	−0.15
2010–1970	−0.01	−0.35	−0.55	−0.01	−0.21	−0.33
Five decades						
2010–1960	0.00	−0.39	−0.26	0.00	−0.23	−0.16

Table 5
Estimated Effect of Prison on Crime, World Panel

	Robbery	Homicide	Auto Theft	In (Robbery)	In (Homicide)	In (auto theft)
	Dependent variable is crime per 100,000 population					
Incarceration rate	0.028	−0.010	−0.336			
	(0.028)	(0.002)	(0.102)			
In (Incarceration rate)				0.312	−0.333	−0.232
				(0.078)	(0.043)	(0.077)
Adjusted R²	−0.054	−0.015	−0.044	−0.028	0.043	−0.048
Observations	649	591	529	649	591	529

Note: Standard errors in parentheses.

We also estimate the log difference regression

$$(5) \qquad C_{ct} - C_{ct-s} = \beta(Q_{ct} - Q_{ct-s}) + \mu_{ct}$$

as a function of the lag length, s. These results are in Figure 5, with the solid lines representing point estimates and the dashed lines the 95 percent confidence intervals. Table 7 lists the number of observations each country contributes to the regressions.

On a priori grounds, we prefer these results to those of Table 5 because they focus on long-run differences, which are less affected by the mechanical relationship between incarceration and crime. However, the results of this empirical exercise are difficult to interpret because of the differing composition of countries. Nonetheless, bracketing the issue on composition, some conclusions may be drawn. First, for homicide and auto theft, the short-run estimates tend to be more positive than those 5 to 10 years out. This is somewhat consistent with a deterrence hypothesis, with the short-run estimates contaminated by the short-run reduction in the flow rate into prison. As discussed above, this effect exerts a positive bias on the estimated coefficients. However, the same tendency is not present for robbery, warning against strong interpretation. Second, after 20 years, according to the data, incarceration tends to have much smaller negative effects—and possibly large and positive effects—on

Table 6
Distribution of Country Observations for
Regressions of Table 5

Country	Dependent Variable			First Year of Data
	Robbery	Homicide	Auto Theft	
United States	41	41	41	1970
Canada	39	39	15	1970
England & Wales	41	41	41	1970
Australia	24	17	15	1982
Austria	13	16	15	1994
Belgium	10	10	10	2000
Bulgaria	27	32	15	1970
Croatia	11	11	10	1994
Czech Republic	17	1	17	1993
Denmark	17	17	17	1993
Estonia	14	16	17	1993
Finland	23	17	17	1987
France	13	16	16	1994
Greece	15	15	12	1993
Hungary	26	17	17	1982
Ireland	10	16	17	1993
Italy	17	17	17	1993
Japan	26	15	13	1980
Latvia	15	15	15	1995
Lithuania	17	17	17	1993
Macedonia	13	9	9	1990
Netherlands	21	16	17	1987
New Zealand	15	15	15	1994
Northern Ireland	17	16	17	1993
Norway	17	17	17	1993

(continued)

Table 6
(continued)

Country	Robbery	Homicide	Auto Theft	First Year of Data
	Dependent Variable			
Poland	17	17	17	1993
Russia	12	12	9	1994
Scotland	26	17	17	1982
Serbia	8	8	8	2002
Slovenia	17	15	16	1993
South Africa	14	14	14	1994
Sweden	23	17	17	1987
Switzerland	17	16	1	1993
Turkey	16	16	16	1993
Total observations	649	591	529	

Source: See text, p. 171.

Figure 5
World Panel Log Difference Regressions

A. Homicide Rate

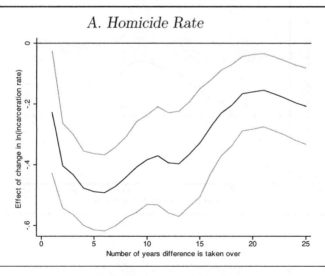

Figure 5
(continued)

B. Auto Theft Rate

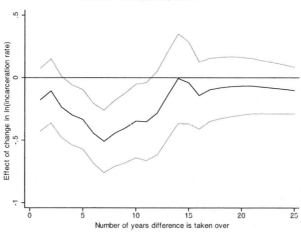

C. Robbery Rate

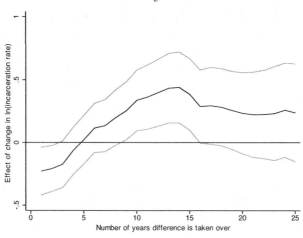

Table 7
Distribution of Country Observations for
Regressions of Figure 5

	Robbery		Homicide		Auto Theft	
	Dependent variable and number of years over which difference is taken					
Country	1 year	10 years	1 year	10 years	1 year	10 years
United States	40	31	40	31	40	31
Canada	37	29	37	29	0	0
England & Wales	40	31	40	31	40	31
Australia	20	13	16	7	14	5
Austria	12	3	15	6	6	5
Belgium	9	0	9	0	9	0
Bulgaria	23	17	23	22	14	5
Croatia	9	1	9	1	9	0
Czech Republic	16	7	0	0	0	7
Denmark	16	7	16	7	16	7
Estonia	12	5	15	6	16	7
Finland	22	13	16	7	16	7
France	12	3	15	6	15	5
Greece	14	5	14	5	5	2
Hungary	23	16	16	7	16	7
Ireland	9	0	15	6	6	7
Italy	16	7	16	7	16	7
Japan	22	16	14	5	12	3
Latvia	14	5	14	5	5	5
Lithuania	16	7	16	7	16	7
Macedonia	10	3	8	0	8	0
Netherlands	19	11	15	6	16	7
New Zealand	14	5	14	5	14	6
Northern Ireland	16	7	15	6	16	7
Norway	16	7	16	7	16	7
Poland	16	7	16	7	16	7
Russia	11	2	11	2	2	0
Scotland	23	16	16	7	16	7
Serbia	7	0	7	0	7	0
Slovenia	16	7	14	5	15	6
South Africa	13	4	13	4	4	4
Sweden	22	13	16	7	16	7
Switzerland	16	7	15	6	6	0
Turkey	15	6	15	6	15	6
Total observations	596	311	547	263	496	212

Source: See text, p. 171.

crime. For homicide, the long-run estimate is approximately -0.20. For auto theft, it is close to -0.10, and for robbery it is roughly 0.25. This is potentially consistent with short-run deterrence effects that are negative and general equilibrium effects that are positive. Overall, however, we caution against strong interpretation based on the regression estimates.

5. CONCLUSION

Since the data are not definitive, a natural question is whether there is evidence against a stark prior. An example of such a stark prior is one that posits no general equilibrium effects and large deterrence effects of punishment. We see three key problems with such an interpretation of the data. First, while in the 1990–2010 period incarceration was generally on the rise in the United States and crime was on the decline, incarceration was rising faster in the 1970–1990 period and no decline in crime was evident. Indeed, crime was rising. Of course, the increase in crime may well have been the impetus for the increased sentences that led to higher incarceration rates.

Second, however, U.S. fluctuations in crime rates are not without peer. Figure 2 indicates that Canadian crime, particularly homicide and robbery, has turning points similar to the U.S. series. This is despite the fact that Canadian incarceration rates are essentially flat over the last 40 years. While Canadian auto theft's turning point is roughly five to seven years after that of the United States, the turning point for England and Wales is essentially the same. However, homicide and robbery in England and Wales turn 10–12 years after they do in the United States. In all three countries, crime is on the decline for all three of these crime types in recent years. This indicates that it is not necessary to have an explosive expansion in prison capacity to see major crime declines, since neither Canada nor England and Wales expanded their prison capacity, yet they eventually saw crime declines.

Third, the timing of the story works poorly. As noted above, an increase in sentence lengths takes some time to work its way through to increases in prison population. Using an example in which we calibrate to U.S. data in 1970, we show that the "python" is not done "swallowing the pig" even after a decade: sentence lengths affect prison populations with a long lag. This implies that the increase in prison population between 1990 and 2000, say, was likely the result of changes to sentencing policy put in place in 1980–85. However, the data contain little evidence of this timing.

Overall, we can hardly doubt that, ceteris paribus, an increase today in the sentence length confronting a potential offender does not have a positive influence on the probability that a nonincarcerated person will commit a crime. This channel would weakly reduce crime. We certainly do not doubt that the same increase in the sentence length would lead to increases in prison stays for those who do elect to commit crime. However, we are not persuaded that these are the only two relevant effects of a shift in punishment policy on the aggregate crime rate. Future work should focus on research designs capable of teasing out these important, but elusive, mechanisms.

REFERENCES

Burdett, Kenneth, Ricardo Lagos, and Randall Wright. 2004. "An On-the-Job Search Model of Crime, Inequality, and Unemployment." *International Economic Review* 45 (3): 681–706.

Doob, Anthony N., and Cheryl Marie Webster. 2006. "Countering Punitiveness: Understanding Stability in Canada's Imprisonment Rate." *Law and Society Review* 40 (2): 325–67.

Freeman, Richard B. 1999. "The Economics of Crime." In *Handbook of Labor Economics*, Vol. 3C, eds. Orley Ashenfelter and David E. Card. New York: Elsevier-North Holland.

McCrary, Justin. 2009. "Dynamic Perspectives on Crime." In *Handbook of the Economics of Crime*, ed. Bruce Benson. Northampton, MA: Edward Elgar.

Rasmusen, Eric. 1996. "Stigma and Self-Fulfilling Expectations of Criminality." *Journal of Law and Economics* 39 (2): 519–44.

Walmsley, Roy. 2009. *The World Prison Population List*, 8th ed. Essex, UK: International Centre for Prison Studies.

Comment

Steven N. Durlauf

Justin McCrary and Sarath Sanga's paper represents an ambitious effort to identify the general equilibrium effects of imprisonment without the use of a structural model but rather through comparisons of similar polities with very dissimilar imprisonment rates. Methodologically, the paper makes two contributions: First, it provides a careful delineation of the distinction between the transition and steady-state empirical relationship between imprisonment rates and crime rates. Second, the paper uses cross-country comparisons to allow for a difference-in-difference strategy to evaluate the effects of imprisonment on crime and so avoids reliance on a structural model. This second idea constitutes the conceptual basis of the paper. As such, this second methodological contribution is tied to current debates in empirical economics and econometrics about the role of economic theory in empirical work.

My discussion will focus on the second contribution because the paper only succeeds to the extent that the cross-country comparison strategy does in fact produce estimates of general equilibrium effects. I will argue that the strategy fails in this respect. In doing so, let me be clear at the start that this is an ambitious and carefully executed analysis of a difficult and policy-relevant problem. The authors' analysis represents a first step in a longer research program. For this reason, while my comments will be critical, they should not be construed as suggesting that the research program be abandoned. Rather, I believe that there may well be a useful role for analyses of the type the authors pursue.

In the discussion, I will refer only to comparisons between the

Steven N. Durlauf is the Vilas Research Professor and the Kenneth J. Arrow Professor of Economics at the University of Wisconsin, Madison. He is a research associate of the National Bureau of Economic Research.

United States and Canada and England and Wales. The criticisms I make apply a fortiori to comparisons between the United States and other countries that appear in the paper.

IS THIS FORM OF ANALYSIS APPROPRIATE?

The first criticism I have with the authors' empirical strategy concerns the assumption that the polities under study are so similar that bivariate imprisonment crime relationships can be revealed by a difference-in-difference strategy. The thought experiment behind the paper is well encapsulated in McCrary and Sanga's statement, "We pay particularly close attention to Canada and England and Wales, as these are natural comparisons for the United States." How is this (asserted) comparability exploited in the empirical exercises? Determinants of crime rates and imprisonment rates that are not due to differences in sanction regimes are "canceled out" in the cross-polity differences. This cancellation plays a role for both series. First, it eliminates factors other than the sanction regime that determine crime. Second, it purges aspects of imprisonment that may be unrelated to the sanction regime difference. However, in my view it is hard to conclude that the difference-in-difference approach is credible in producing interpretable, policy-relevant information on punishment and crime rates.

First, the authors do not make an adequate case that the United States, Canada, and England and Wales are sufficiently similar that the only difference between them is that the United States imposes harsher penalties than the other two polities. The question is not whether the three polities are similar, but whether one can argue that they are comparable in a way that justifies the authors' interpretation that a comparison of the difference in crime rates and imprisonment rates yields evidence of "the" effect of imprisonment on crime. In some sense, the authors are in great trouble in making such an assumption because of the data series they have chosen to study: U.S. crime and imprisonment rates are quite different from Canada and England and Wales, so it is obvious that one has to make an argument that comparability holds along the dimensions needed for this particular study. Two pieces of evidence are presented in favor of comparability. Figures 2B and 2D and 4B and 4D show that if one rescales the homicide and robbery rates for the United States versus Canada and the United States versus England and Wales, both pairs of series appear to move together. Second, there is a high correlation, 0.86, between the U.S. and Canadian homicide rates. Leaving aside the failure to provide a comparable statistic for robberies and the confused discussion of trends (the term is not defined and it is not clear what the authors mean when they distinguish trends and levels; in time series analysis one distinguishes trends and *cycles*), neither of these pieces of evidence really tells us anything about comparability. One reason is statistical: it has long been known that spurious correlations can be found between time series with temporal dependence (Granger and Newbold 1974). So neither piece of evidence is, on its face, informative about actual similarities in the countries. Second, the fact that the crime series for two polities move together is consistent with the coexistence of common and idiosyncratic determinants of the series. It does not mean that the polities react similarly to a given variable such as imprisonment policy.

This comparability problem has plagued the cross-country growth literature. Evidence of coefficient heterogeneity, nonlinearity, and residual region-specific heterogeneity have all proven to be of first-order importance in understanding cross-country growth patterns; see Brock and Durlauf (2001) and Durlauf, Johnson, and Temple (2006) for elaboration. Given the checkered history of empirical claims based on cross-country growth regressions (many of which evaporate when comparability assumptions are relaxed), concern about comparability issues for cross-country analyses of crime and imprisonment is only natural. The authors need to provide a credible justification as to why their differencing strategy is adequate for the questions they wish to answer rather than simply relying on conventional wisdom that the United States, Canada, and England and Wales are similar in a manner that renders the authors' empirical strategy valid or using a simple correlation to justify the implicit exchangeability assumption they are making. (See Brock and Durlauf (2001) for a discussion of exchangeability, which is the statistical formalization of the comparability notion used in this paper.)

The cross-country growth literature can in fact be used to illustrate why the authors' empirical strategy is problematic. The use of log differences in this paper can be interpreted as comparing $\Delta \log CRIME_{U.S.} - \Delta \log CRIME_{other}$ to $\Delta \log IMPRISONMENT_{U.S.} - \Delta \log IMPRISONMENT_{other}$. Suppose one asked the following cross-country growth question: What is the effect of a country's savings rate on its growth rate? If one were to use the methodology of this paper, one would answer the question by comparing $\Delta\log INCOME_{U.S.}$ − $\Delta\log INCOME_{other}$ to $\Delta\log SAVINGS_{U.S.}$ − $\Delta\log SAVINGS_{other}$. However, this would make little sense even if data were restricted to similar countries; for example, the United States, Canada, and England and Wales. Why? The Solow growth model (a useful baseline) implies that growth is determined by initial income and population growth; augmentations of the model would include factors such as monetary and fiscal policy, all of which differ across countries. Note that if the question were the effect of a physical capital savings rate, one would be assuming that the effects of the human capital savings rates are canceled out. The problem is that comparability in the loose form that is documented in the paper does not mean that the difference in growth rates can be attributed to differences in a single variable.

A possible authors' rejoinder is that the imprisonment difference swamps other differences between the United States and Canada or England and Wales as pertains to imprisonment and crime. But this is not obvious unless one knows how the other variables affect crime. Further, there are good reasons to question comparability as it is used here. One obvious source is differences in the time series for unemployment, output, etc., which presumably bear upon crime. In Durlauf (1989), I found that the difference between per capita output for the United States and Canada under a second order autoregression specification produced coefficients that summed to 0.95, and the difference between the United States and the United Kingdom under a second order autoregression specification produced coefficients that summed to 0.83. Standard errors were large enough that one could conclude there were unit roots. Similar results have subsequently appeared in the years since.

I believe this lack of comparability likely also reflects cultural factors involved in "American exceptionalism." Personally, I think that economic models of crime ignore the moral dimension to criminal behavior, which in my judgment is something other than a claim about the disutility of immoral actions. I further think that most social scientists would agree that there are complex cultural reasons why immoral behaviors (e.g., crime) can differ across countries. Whether or not one agrees with my view that preference heterogeneity cannot accommodate the moral aspects of individual choice, many attitudinal differences can easily be identified among the three polities the authors study in the World Value Survey (Inglehart et al.

2010). I do not delineate these because their relationship to crime is not clear. For example, Americans are far more religious than Canadians or the British (Inglehart et al. do not break out England and Wales).[1] That would seem inconsistent with the high American crime rates. But if one considers oppositional culture ideas (e.g., Ogbu 2003), which have been applied to understand black/white educational differences to socioeconomic groups, one can imagine that, given the value society places on success, those who are not well off may react by rejecting mainstream ethical norms. Obviously, this is speculative. My argument is that the authors do not have a theory of why cultural differences on crime-relevant dimensions do not constitute confounders that invalidate the conceptual basis of their thought experiment.

PRIMACY OF THE SANCTION REGIME

My second criticism is that McCrary and Sanga's paper does not establish that the estimated imprisonment rate effects are policy-relevant. The authors recognize that natural variation in incarceration rates occurs for multiple reasons, writing, "These estimates indicate there are often quite violent swings in crime rates that have little to do with penal policy." I would go further. The imprisonment rate is an endogenous variable, so all the calculations in this paper involve comparing differences in endogenous variables. It is unclear how the calculations should affect our thinking about criminal justice policy. The policy-relevant object for assessing criminal justice policy is the *sanction regime*, which determines both the crime and imprisonment rates. Sanction regimes are usually specified in terms of the probability of apprehension and severity of punishment. Blumstein and Nagin (1978) showed that in a steady state, the relationship between crime rates and imprisonment rates is not constrained by deterrence theory in the sense that a change in the sanction regime can either raise imprisonment and lower crime or lower both imprisonment and crime; the effect depends on the elasticity of the crime rate with respect to certainty and severity. The McCrary

---

[1] On a 1–10 scale, with 10 meaning very important, 26 percent of the British, 49 percent of Canadians, and 58 percent of Americans answered 9 or 10 to the question, "How important is God in your Life?" in 2006. These differences are qualitatively similar for other years (Inglehart et al. 2010, 246).

and Sanga simulation results suggest the same is true for transitions. The authors are in essence regressing endogenous variables against endogenous variables and relying on the interpretation of coefficient values at different horizons in the differences to tell a story about policy. This is not uninteresting, but it does not indicate what substantive information is revealed in the calculations. The Blumstein and Nagin result illustrates why one cannot make facile claims as to what is learned from comparing imprisonment and crime rates. For this reason, McCrary and Sanga's title is misleading. The concept of a general equilibrium effect of imprisonment on crime is as conceptually ill-posed as the concept of a general equilibrium effect of prices on output levels. A well-posed concept is the general equilibrium effect on both imprisonment and crime of an exogenous change in the sanction regime.

Once one considers the complexities involved in describing a sanction regime, the interpretability of the authors' results is further muddied. Actual sanction regimes will involve distributions of penalties as functions of offender characteristics, including past offenses. A "three-strikes" policy is very different from a policy of automatic imprisonment for a first felony. I believe that U.S. imprisonment policy is inefficient in terms of maximizing deterrence for a steady-state imprisonment rate. (Durlauf and Nagin 2011a and 2011b conclude that three-strikes policies should not be continued for cost-benefit reasons, for example.) But nothing in the exercises done in this paper would let me draw policy-relevant conclusions of this type.

The limitations of the substantive conclusions one can draw are inherent in the atheoretical empirical strategy the authors have chosen. Some explicit description of the process by which individuals make the choice to commit a crime is needed to produce interpretable results. The statistical exercises produce evidence on long-run relationships between endogenous variables; but without a behavioral framework, the relevance of the evidence to the question of how different sanction regimes affect imprisonment and crime is unclear. And this question is precisely the one that is relevant to policy.

FUTURE WORK

These criticisms do not imply that McCrary and Sanga's exercises fail to provide insights that may be useful in policy evaluation. Vector autoregression and cointegration analyses are purely statistical methods that have produced important insights in macroeconomics. Understanding the strengths and limitations of these methods took years of research and debate.

McCrary and Sanga have launched a research program. It is easy to raise objections at this early stage of their work. My remarks do not imply that they are on the wrong track. Hence, while I do reject the claim that this paper has produced credible general equilibrium estimates of the different effects of alternative sanction regimes on crime, on the research program I conclude with the Scottish verdict "Not Proven." When evaluated against theoretical models of crime so that the informational content of the exercises is better understood, the research program may prove to be a useful contribution to the abductive analysis of sanction policy.

REFERENCES

Blumstein, Alfred, and Daniel Nagin. 1978. "On the Optimal Use of Incarceration." *Operations Research* 26: 381–405.

Brock, William, and Steven Durlauf. 2001. "Growth Empirics and Reality." *World Bank Economic Review* 15: 229–72.

Durlauf, Steven. 1989. "Output Persistence, Economic Structure, and the Choice of Stabilization Policy." *Brookings Papers on Economic Activity* 2: 69–116.

Durlauf, Steven, Paul Johnson, and Jonathan Temple. 2006. "Growth Econometrics." In *Handbook of Economic Growth,* eds. Philippe Aghion and Steven Durlauf. Amsterdam: North-Holland.

Durlauf, Steven, and Daniel Nagin. 2011a. "Imprisonment and Crime: Can Both Be Reduced?" *Criminology and Public Policy* 10: 13–54.

Durlauf, Steven, and Daniel Nagin. 2011b. "The Deterrent Effect of Imprisonment." In *Controlling Crime,* eds. Philip Cook, Jens Ludwig, and Justin McCrary. Chicago: University of Chicago Press.

Granger, Clive, and Paul Newbold. 1974. "Spurious Regressions in Econometrics." *Journal of Econometrics* 2: 111–20.

Inglehart, Ronald, et al. 2010. *Changing Human Beliefs and Values.* Romero de Terreros, Mexico: Siglo XII.

Ogbu, John. 2003. *Black Students in an Affluent Suburb.* Mahwah NJ: Lawrence Erlbaum Associates.

Comment

Bruce Sacerdote

Justin McCrary and Sarath Sanga present an innovative paper on a critical public policy topic. The authors are pursuing a very big question, namely whether the large U.S. expansion in incarceration rates over the past few decades paid off in terms of reduced crime. The United States had a large increase in incarceration beginning in the 1980s, which accompanied a massive crime wave. Crime began to subside in the mid-1990s and continues to fall. It is tempting to attribute some or all of the drop in the crime rate to increased incarceration. But as the authors show, this is not a simple causal relationship; crime, sentence length, and imprisonment are all endogenous variables within a complex system. The authors note that other countries experienced similarly timed rises and falls in crime without the expansion of imprisonment.

The authors' hope is to construct a difference-in-differences estimate, which takes the United States/Canada (or United States/ England and Wales) log differences in the crime rate over long time periods and divides by the log differences in the incarceration rate. This is intended to capture the effects of changes in incarceration on crime. Subtracting out the changes for the comparison country (Canada or England and Wales) is supposed to remove general time trends that are common to both countries but that are unrelated to incarceration policy.

McCrary and Sanga's paper assumes that the big run-up in incarceration rates is a policy shift that is largely exogenous to crime. They present a plausible argument for this and, if the shift is exogenous to the crime and punishment system of equations, they may be able to identify the effect of imprisonment on crime.

Bruce Sacerdote holds the Richard S. Braddock 1963 Professorship in Economics at Dartmouth College and is a research associate of the National Bureau of Economic Research.

The authors' object of interest is how crime responds to the sentence length. Because a long time series of average sentence lengths is hard to construct, the authors use the actual incarceration rate as a proxy for the severity of sentence lengths. The paper includes a very nice section on how the dynamics of crime (C) and incarceration (Q) would evolve in response to an exogenous shift in sentence length (S). The bottom line from this analysis is that in the presence of deterrence, calculating $\Delta \ln C / \Delta \ln Q$, will tend to overstate the true elasticity of crime with respect to sentence length. Both discussants agreed that working out the dynamics of this problem is a nice contribution to the literature.

The authors conclude that there is little evidence that crime fell in the United States in response to increased incarceration rates. However, it's important to recognize that the results depend greatly on which log difference is used and which crime rate (murder, auto theft, robbery, etc.) is used. For example, the 1970–2010 differences for motor vehicle theft show big drops in crime associated with big increases in incarceration. Mechanically, this is because, relative to its base value, auto theft fell by 10 times as much in the United States as it did in Canada. The audience and the other discussant encouraged the authors to add standard errors to their point estimates, which seems like a sensible idea.

My first suggestion for the authors is to attempt to distinguish among imprisonment regimes for various crimes in the analysis. If 40 percent of the run-up in imprisonment in the United States is for drug-related crimes, then separating those from other crimes may affect the results. Admittedly, drug crimes are often comingled with robbery, assault, etc., so this is not a clean or clear-cut task. But given the importance of big shifts in narcotics policy in explaining the run-up in imprisonment, this issue ought to be addressed. The data might show, for example, that auto thefts responded to auto theft sentences.

My second suggestion is to consider measuring expected sentence length directly rather than using incarceration rates as a proxy. Again, the availability of data is a big issue, but using sentencing data directly would make measuring the elasticity of crime with respect to sentence length easier and would remove one of the endogeneity problems.

This leads to my third point, which brings out the great strengths and weaknesses of the paper. This is essentially a macro paper written on a question for which we have traditionally used micro evidence. The authors already have a series of excellent papers using local identification to get at the deterrence effects of enhanced sentences. Specifically, McCrary and Lee (2009) and McCrary and Sanga (2011) use the discontinuity in expected sentence that occurs when offenders turn "the age of majority." That is, expected sentence length increases when a potential offender turns 16, 17, or 18 years old. And since states have actually altered those laws, there is not only significant discontinuity in expected sentence, but exogenous shifts in the point in the age distribution where that discontinuity is located.

More broadly, it may be possible to identify other exogenous shifts in sentence length at the state, local, or crime-specific level. For example, Kuziemko (forthcoming) uses a large prison release in Georgia to identify the effects of actual sentence length on recidivism. Kessler and Levitt (1999) suggest that the implementation of sentence enhancement laws could be useful for identifying deterrence effects. These sorts of identification strategies allow one to hone in on the effect of interest with less worry about differential trends in unobservables or the endogeneity of incarceration and crime driving the results.

McCrary and Sanga take a much bigger-picture approach, which is potentially good—we might miss the forest for the trees if we look at too narrow a source of local identification. And I agree with the authors that it is useful at least to ask whether the broad time trend in incarceration and crime can help explain whether incarceration reduces crime. The downside of the big-picture/macro approach is its reliance on strong assumptions (e.g., the increase in incarceration is an exogenous policy change) and the potential for confounding factors to invalidate the analysis.

One such confounding factor might be the crack epidemic of the 1980s and 1990s (see Fryer, Heaton, Levitt, and Murphy, forthcoming). As mentioned above, a large portion of the run-up in imprisonment was for drug-related crimes, which are counted in the imprisonment statistics but not necessarily the crime statistics in the authors' macro analysis. During discussion of the paper, many people mentioned prosecutorial discretion and the fact that many crimes are interrelated. Police and prosecutors may simply pursue the most convenient charge or the one with the stiffest penalty. If all crack crimes are connected with "index" crimes, then the authors' approach is a very useful one and gets around this inability to separate crimes cleanly.

Overall, I found this paper to be a useful exercise, even though it did not shift my priors as much as the authors' related work on deterrence using micro data. I appreciate that in the current paper the authors attempt to capture both deterrence and incapacitation effects, especially given that we seem to have many clever micro identification strategies to measure deterrence and few to measure incapacitation.

REFERENCES

Fryer, Roland, Paul Heaton, Steven Levitt, and Kevin Murphy. Forthcoming. "Measuring the Impact of Crack Cocaine." *Economic Inquiry.*

Kessler, Daniel, and Steven D. Levitt. 1999. "Using Sentence Enhancements to Distinguish between Deterrence and Incapacitation." *Journal of Law and Economics* 42 (S1): 343–64.

Kuziemko, Ilyana. Forthcoming. "How Should Inmates Be Released from Prison? An Assessment of Parole versus Fixed-Sentence Regimes." *Quarterly Journal of Economics* 128 (1).

McCrary, Justin, and David Lee. 2009. "The Deterrence Effect of Prison: Dynamic Theory and Evidence." Working paper. University of California, Berkeley, and Princeton University.

McCrary, Justin, and Sarath Sanga. 2011. "Youth Offenders and the Deterrence Effect of Prison." Working paper. University of California, Berkeley, and Yale Law School.

Cato Institute

Founded in 1977, the Cato Institute is a public policy research foundation dedicated to broadening the parameters of policy debate to allow consideration of more options that are consistent with the traditional American principles of limited government, individual liberty, and peace. To that end, the Institute strives to achieve greater involvement of the intelligent, concerned lay public in questions of policy and the proper role of government.

The Institute is named for *Cato's Letters*, libertarian pamphlets that were widely read in the American Colonies in the early 18th century and played a major role in laying the philosophical foundation for the American Revolution.

Despite the achievement of the nation's Founders, today virtually no aspect of life is free from government encroachment. A pervasive intolerance for individual rights is shown by government's arbitrary intrusions into private economic transactions and its disregard for civil liberties.

To counter that trend, the Cato Institute undertakes an extensive publications program that addresses the complete spectrum of policy issues. Books, monographs, and shorter studies are commissioned to examine the federal budget, Social Security, regulation, military spending, international trade, and myriad other issues. Major policy conferences are held throughout the year, from which papers are published thrice yearly in the *Cato Journal*. The Institute also publishes the quarterly magazine *Regulation*.

In order to maintain its independence, the Cato Institute accepts no government funding. Contributions are received from foundations, corporations, and individuals, and other revenue is generated from the sale of publications. The Institute is a nonprofit, tax-exempt, educational foundation under Section 501(c)3 of the Internal Revenue Code.

CATO INSTITUTE
1000 Massachusetts Ave., N.W.
Washington, D.C. 20001
www.cato.org